T0289941

Corporate Governance System of Japanese Multinational Companies

A Quantitative Evaluation

Corporate Governance System of Japanese Multinational Companies

A Quantitative Evaluation

Dipak Basu
Nagasaki University, Japan

Victoria Miroshnik
Reitaku University, Japan

 **World Scientific**

NEW JERSEY · LONDON · SINGAPORE · BEIJING · SHANGHAI · HONG KONG · TAIPEI · CHENNAI · TOKYO

Published by

World Scientific Publishing Co. Pte. Ltd.

5 Toh Tuck Link, Singapore 596224

USA office: 27 Warren Street, Suite 401-402, Hackensack, NJ 07601

UK office: 57 Shelton Street, Covent Garden, London WC2H 9HE

Library of Congress Cataloging-in-Publication Data

Names: Basu, Dipak R., author. | Miroshnik, Victoria, 1969–   author.
Title: Corporate governance system of Japanese multinational companies : a quantitative evaluation /
    Dipak Basu (Nagasaki University, Japan) and Victoria Miroshnik (Reitaku University, Japan).
Description: New Jersey : World Scientific, 2019.
Identifiers: LCCN 2018043523 | ISBN 9789813276079 (hc : alk. paper)
Subjects: LCSH: International business enterprises--Japan--Management. |
    Corporate governance--Japan.
Classification: LCC HD2907 .B369 2019 | DDC 338.60952--dc23
LC record available at https://lccn.loc.gov/2018043523

British Library Cataloguing-in-Publication Data
A catalogue record for this book is available from the British Library.

For any available supplementary material, please visit
https://www.worldscientific.com/worldscibooks/10.1142/11150#t=suppl

Desk Editors: Dr. Sree Meenakshi Sajani/Sandhya Venkatesh

Typeset by Stallion Press
Email: enquiries@stallionpress.com

Printed in Singapore

To

Professor Makoto Takashima,
who opened the door of Japan to us

Preface

We went to Japan to explore the Japanese civilization which has accepted Buddhism from India and provided support for the independence movement of India. We have passionate interest in Japanese history, art, literature, and politics.

When we went back to our countries, India and Russia, people were surprised to know how Japanese people are. They thought that we were not being truthful. It cannot be, but it is. Japanese people are the most kind, most polite people who are always ready to help.

In the beginning, we started writing about Japan's foreign investment. Then we came across Professor Shigeru Uchida, who introduced us and accompanied us to all major automobile companies and their most senior executives. That was the beginning of our research on the Japanese management system.

Japanese management system is unique and it is based on its culture of respect for all people without any distinction. We were amazed to see that senior executives stand in the queue with ordinary workers and sit on the same tables to have their lunch. It is unthinkable in other countries of the world. We were told by some British executives in a Japanese automobile company that this is the culture and those could not conform to it must go away.

In Thailand, one very senior Thai executive told us that the Japanese system of management corresponds to the Buddhist religion and culture of Thailand. In India, one senior executive who came from Kerala, the state ruled by the Communists at that time, said that the Japanese management system is the real socialism. Thus, people from other parts of the world have tried to adopt the Japanese system in their own way.

This book is about the corporate governance system which in other books is described as a set of rules and regulations regarding the relationship of the executives and the shareholders. In this book, we have taken a different approach. Corporate governance system creates a culture, which creates a set of values that direct the organization for the benefits of the stake holders. Workers together compose a major stake holder.

How to quantify these issues is the main concern, because without quantification, nothing concrete will emerge. This book is an attempt to quantify the corporate governance system of major Japanese companies.

The purpose of this book is to study an unexplored area of corporate governance. We are trying to examine whether corporate governance system can be affected by the organizational culture, leader culture, and the operations management system in general. In addition, we like to know whether a specific corporate governance system can affect the organizational culture and operations management system and create a different type of leader culture. We have studied in depth, some major Japanese multinational companies and compare their corporate governance system at home (in Japan) and in host countries like Britain, India, and Thailand. We have conducted a series of in-depth interviews of the senior executives of major Japanese multinational companies and surveys of opinion to construct quantitative models for Japan, Thailand, and India to analyze these propositions mentioned above.

About the Authors

Dipak Basu is currently an Emeritus Professor of International Economics in Nagasaki University. Previously, he was a Lecturer in the Institute of Agricultural Economics of Oxford University, Research officer in the Department of Applied Economics of Cambridge University, Senior Economist in charge of the Middle East & Africa division of Standard & Poor's, and Senior Economist in the Ministry of Foreign Affairs of Saudi Arabia. He is a member of the editorial board of *International Journal of Decision Sciences*, *Risk and Management*, and was the editor (1986–1988) of the *Middle East & Africa Review*. He received his PhD from the University of Birmingham, UK.

Victoria Miroshnik is currently an Associate Professor of Management in Tokyo International University. Previously, she was an Associate Professor at the American University in Dubai, Ritsumeikan Asia Pacific University in Japan, and Keimyung University in South Korea. She received her PhD from the University of Glasgow, UK. Her previous books are *Corporate Culture in Multinationals Companies* and *Organizational Culture and Commitment*.

Contents

List of Figures

Chapter 8

List of Tables

Chapter 1

Purpose of a Business Corporation

The purpose of a corporation in Japan differs from that in the West. While the latter is aimed primarily to provide profits for shareholders, Japanese corporations exist fundamentally to produce economic value to Japan as a nation. Creation of employment to the Japanese people is the highest priority of the Japanese corporations. Given this difference in corporate purpose, Western i.e., Anglo-American notions of corporate governance have limited applicability in Japan. While the West emphasizes the relationship between shareholders, management, and the Board of Directors, Japanese corporations are dedicated to their stakeholders, i.e., the employees, customers, suppliers, creditors, and community.

However, Japanese corporations may be following the much older style of American corporate governance. It was only in the 1960s and 1970s that the voice of shareholders started to gain prominence in corporate governance in the United States. Most U.S. boards 30 or 40 years ago looked rather similar to what Japanese boards look like now in terms of independent outside directors. There are diversities of corporate governance practices among U.S. companies. Some adhere to practices that are radical by Japanese standards (e.g., IBM Corp. and Dell Computer Corp., whose boards comprise all outside members except for one), whereas some do not look too dissimilar to the typical Japanese pattern. Similarly, there are diversities of corporate governance practices among Japanese companies. Most progressive Japanese companies may be more open than the most conservative U.S. companies. It is expected that there will be a certain amount of convergence of Japanese corporate governance practices to the U.S. model as globalization proceeds and international accounting standards are being adopted in Japanese companies increasingly. However, given the deeply rooted differences in the role, behaviour, and function of corporations in the two countries, it may take decades, before corporate governance in Japan converges to that in the United States.

Chapter 2

Traditional Practices of Corporate Governance in Japan

The corporate governance of Japanese companies is often described as "Contingent Governance" or "Emergency Governance". This implies that the management are quite free in their day-to-day operations, but in a crisis situation, the main banks take over the management. This structure is supported by three major features (Yasui, 1999). These are as follows:

(1) homogeneous and hierarchical Board of Directors;
(2) silent shareholders;
(3) monitoring by banks.

Homogeneous and Hierarchical Board of Directors

The boards are composed of homogenous members of similar nationality and have a hierarchical structure. These boards have some similarity with the boards in US companies, but there are significant differences. In the USA, directors are appointed from outside in most cases. There is also diversity of national and cultural origin. In Japan, most of the members are inside men. They have many years of experience of working within the same organization.

This has serious effects on the management of the company. In the USA, the boards appoint CEOs and other senior officers. In Japanese

3

companies, the board members are responsible for most important management decision-making. In the Japanese framework, the supervisory function of the board is supported by the corporate auditors. According to "The Commercial Code" of Japan, the corporate auditors, who also supervise corporate affairs, are appointed by shareholders. However, in practice, they only check the legality of the affairs of the management. Also, most corporate auditors are ex-employees of the same company or from partner companies.

Silent Shareholders

In most Japanese companies, a significant portion of shares is held by important banks, insurance companies and members of the same *Keiretsu* group. The prevailing culture is the cross-shareholding by other Japanese companies. Thus, there is no such thing like hostile take over. Shareholders do not interfere in the management of the company to maintain harmony, which is the guiding principle of the Japanese corporate affair.

Monitoring by Banks

Japanese firms depend significantly on banks for the financing of daily working costs and investment, and banks are in a position to control them. It is common in Japan that one of these banks, which maintain financial relationship, acts as the "main bank".

The main bank is the largest creditor for the company and the principal supplier of various financial services and provides management of bond issues. When the company is in distress, the bank would take over the management.

The Role of Employees

Although as in some European countries, the employees' involvement in the corporate governance process in Japan is not legally guaranteed, their influence is often very significant. Satisfaction of the employees' interest is one of the important measures of corporate performance.

This is associated with lifetime employment. The management has to pay proper attention to motivate them to contribute the maximum to the company.

Recent Changes

Japanese firms have recently become less dependent on banks. Japanese corporations can now to raise their required funds from the stock markets. It is no longer a very profitable business for banks to act as the main bank.

The attitude of the shareholders have changed. Foreign investors demand more active participations as the shareholding by domestic corporations has been diminishing significantly. The members of the boards are required to provide better corporate governance, as otherwise they would be responsible for enormous financial liability.

The corporate accounting standards and disclosure requirements are being significantly reformed so as to conform to the requirement of the international stock markets where the Japanese companies are listed.

As a result, the composition of the board is changing as well. Now, many companies try to reduce the number of the members of the boards to turn them as an important decision-making body. Also, a number of companies introduced the executive officer system, separating the board and the management of the company. The function of statutory auditors, legally responsible for supervision over management on behalf of the shareholders, is now increasingly important. The American system of appointments of independent outside directors is introduced in Japanese companies.

Chapter 3

Corporate Governance System in Honda and Sony

In describing the corporate governance system in Japan, we focus mainly on two companies from two sectors, automobiles and consumers' electronics, Honda and Sony.

Honda Philosophy

The corporate philosophy of Honda as given in their website (http://world. honda.com/profile/philosophy) is as follows:

> "Maintaining a global viewpoint, we are dedicated to supplying products of the highest quality at a reasonable price for worldwide customer satisfaction. To meet the particular needs of customers in different regions around the world, we base our sales networks, research & development centers, and manufacturing facilities in each region. Furthermore, as a socially responsible corporate citizen, we strive to address important environmental and safety issues."

Based on this corporate philosophy, the company is enhancing corporate governance as the important part of its management system.

> "Our aim is to have our customers and society, as well as our shareholders and investors, place even greater trust in us and to ensure that Honda is a company that society wants to exist."

External directors and corporate auditors are appointed to the Board of Directors and the Board of Corporate Auditors. They are responsible for the supervision and auditing of the company. Honda also has an operating officer system. Operating officers are under the Board of Directors. Each director is appointed for one year, and their compensation depends on the performance of the company.

Each region has its own headquarters, with a general manager who is also a member of the Board of Directors is in charge. Then there are the management councils and regional operating councils responsible for the management of their respective areas. Each division of the company is responsible for legal and ethical compliance and risk management. Honda's basic policy is to have the appropriate disclosure of company information, financial results on a quarterly basis, and announcement of management strategies.

State of the Company's Management Structure

Management Organization

Board of Directors

The Board of Directors consists of 20 directors, including two outside directors.

The company has appointed outside directors to receive advice on its corporate activities. The Board of Directors also provides information on items of business and topics as necessary to outside directors.

Board of Corporate Auditors

The Board of Corporate Auditors consists of six corporate auditors, including three outside corporate auditors. They attain meetings of the Board of Directors and inspect company's assets and liabilities. The corporate auditors work in collaboration with the audit office, which is responsible for the internal audits. The Board of Directors also provides items of business and other information as necessary to the outside corporate auditors (http://www.honda.co.jp/investors/ in Japanese; http://world.honda.com/investors/).

Accounting Audits

Auditing reports are based on the Commercial Code's Audit Special Exceptions Law (Company Law from fiscal 2007), the Securities and Exchange Law, and the U.S. Securities Exchange Act. They also supervise the independent auditors. Each contracts of the company must have prior consent from the Board of Corporate Auditors.

Business Execution System

Organization

The company has six regional operations around the world. The company has four major business operations, motorcycles, automobiles, power products, and spare parts. Each functional area — such as Customer Service Operations, Production Operations, Purchasing Operations, Business Management Operations, and Business Support Operations — supports the other functional areas. Honda R&D Co. Ltd., is for research and development on products, while Honda Engineering Co. Ltd., is for research and development for the production technology.

Management Council

There is the management council, which consists of 10 representative directors. This management council considers important management issues in collaboration with the Board of Directors.

Regional Operating Councils

Regional operating councils are there at each regional operation to discuss important management issues in the region.

Status of Measures Related to Shareholders and Others with Vested Interests

The company sends convocation notices before the date required by law, and also allows shareholders to exercise their voting rights via the Internet, using personal computers or mobile phones. Convocation notices are sent in English to overseas investors. In these and other ways, the company strives to make the exercise of rights as smooth as possible.

For analysts and institutional investors, the company holds meetings to present its results four times a year and meetings with the president twice a year. Company representatives visit and hold information meetings as needed for major Japanese and overseas institutional investors to explain the Honda Group's future business strategies. Representatives based in North America and Europe also hold information meetings for institutional investors as appropriate. Moreover, the company conducts regular tours of facilities in Japan and overseas for shareholders and other investors (http://www.honda.co.jp/investors/ in Japanese; http://world.honda.com/investors).

Respecting the Perspective of Stakeholders

Honda Group has a set of behavioural guidelines, which individual employees should observe. Honda pursues environmental protection activities and social contribution activities. These reflect the company's effort to enhance its corporate social activities.

Group Governance System

The "Honda Conduct Guideline", formulated to guide the behaviour of all employees, is posted on the company's website (http://world.honda.com/conductguideline/). In addition, each division produces more detailed behavioural guidelines according to its specific attributes.

Self-Assessment Checklist

Each division of the company has a checklist that clarifies specific laws and risks to consider. There is a Compliance Officer, responsible for all compliance-related activities. Business Ethics Committee is chaired by the Compliance Officer and consists of directors and corporate officers. The Committee deliberates matters related to corporate ethics and compliance. It met four times in the year under review.

Business Ethics Improvement Proposal Line

Honda places high priority on open communications in its divisions (https://www.hondamotoreuropelogistics.com/en/core-values/). It encourages employees to suggest improvements on corporate ethics.

Risk Management System

Honda Crisis Response Rules are designed to address company-wide crises, major natural disasters, or any other major issues. The company has appointed a Risk Management Officer. There is also the Company-Wide Response Headquarters to consider actions related to major crisis.

Business Audits

The president directly controls the audit office, which is an independent supervisory department. This office evaluates the performance of each department and suggests practical steps to improve the activities of subsidiaries and affiliates in each region.

Disclosure Committee

The Disclosure Committee is responsible for the accurate disclosure of corporate information and financial reports.

Code of Ethics

Following the "Section 406 of the Sarbanes–Oxley Act of 2002", Honda has also established a "Code of Ethics" to observe the rules of the U.S. Securities and Exchange Commission. Companies listed on the NYSE must comply with certain standards regarding corporate governance under Section 303A of the NYSE Listed Company Manual. However, listed companies that are foreign private issuers, such as Honda, are permitted to follow home country practice *in lieu* of certain provisions of Section 303A.

There are significant differences between the corporate governance practices followed by the U.S. listed companies under Section 303A of the NYSE Listed Company Manual and those followed by Honda.

Corporate Governance Practices Followed by NYSE-listed U.S. Companies

A NYSE-listed U.S. company must have a majority of directors meeting the independence requirements under Section 303A of the NYSE Listed Company Manual.

Under the Japan's company law there are corporate auditors (the "corporate auditor system"), who are independent of management irements under Japan's Company Law (http://world.honda.com/RandD/global/). An outside corporate auditor is someone who has not served as a director, accounting councilor, executive officer, manager, or any other employee of the company or any of its subsidiaries. Currently, Honda has three outside corporate auditors, which constitute 50% of Honda's corporate auditors. A NYSE-listed U.S. company must have an audit committee composed entirely of independent directors, and the audit committee must have at least three members. The main function of the Board of Corporate Auditors is to protect the shareholders.

Japanese companies that employ a corporate auditor system, including Honda, are required to have at least three corporate auditors. Currently, Honda has six corporate auditors. Each corporate auditor has a four-year term. In contrast, the term of each director of Honda is one year.

There has to be, under the laws of the New York stock exchange, a corporate governance committee in every listed company. This committee must be composed of independent directors. Honda's directors are elected at a meeting of shareholders. Its Board of Directors does not have the power to fill vacancies thereon.

Honda's corporate auditors are also elected at a meeting of shareholders. A proposal by Honda's Board of Directors to elect a corporate auditor must be approved by a resolution of its Board of Corporate Auditors. A NYSE-listed U.S. company must have a compensation committee composed entirely of independent directors. Maximum total amounts of compensation for Honda directors and corporate auditors are proposed to, and voted on, by a meeting of shareholders. Once the proposals for such maximum total amounts of compensation are approved at the meeting of shareholders, each of the Board of Directors and Board of Corporate Auditors determines the compensation amount for each member within the respective maximum total amounts.

A NYSE-listed U.S. company must generally obtain shareholder approval with respect to any equity compensation plan. Currently, Honda does not adopt stock option compensation plans. When Honda adopts it, for such plans, Honda must obtain shareholder approval for stock options only if the stock options are issued with specifically favourable conditions or price concerning the issuance and exercise of the stock options.

In Table 1, the situation of the board in Japanese corporations can be summarized as of June 2003. It shows that many companies were actively pursuing corporate governance in 2003.

Table 2 reveals the schedule for account settlement and general meetings in companies listed in the first section of Tokyo Stock Exchange (TSE).

Table 1.   Japanese Board of Directors (as of June, 2003).

	1,516 Companies Out of the Listed Ones in the First Section of TSE	Nikkei 225
Average number of members in the board (Headcount)	11.7	15.5
Average number of outside board members (Commercial Code Article 188) (Headcount)	0.8	1
Number of companies with non-statutory executive officer system	530	113
Number of companies with committees	29	7

Source: Research by Japan Investor Relations and Investor Support, Inc.

Table 2.   Annual general meetings.

	Companies Listed in The First Section of TSE (Note #3)	Nikkei 225
General meeting held on the highest concentration date: June 27, 2002 (number of companies)	906	143
Average number of days from mailing date of notice to general meeting (Note #1)	17.2	19.8
Average number of days from account settlement to the announcement of financial statements (Note #2)	46.3	43.9

Notes: Note #1: Includes meetings held in June 2003 only. Note #2: Although some very short ones were about seven days, the majority was around 50 days. Note #3: Out of the companies listed in the first section of TSE, researched on 1,516 companies.
Source: Research by Japan Investor Relations and Investor Support, Inc.

Institutional investors increasingly seek executives who regard shareholders' stakes more highly and are willing to monitor company operation strictly. Institutional investors think Board of Directors should represent shareholders and the board should be managed by this principle. Although these practices have already been implemented in companies abroad, they have not been common in Japanese companies yet.

Corporate governance is often debated in the context of the old question: Who owns a company? In a U.S.-style company "A company belongs to the shareholders" is the principle, while in a Japanese style company "a company belongs to the employees" is the principle. However, in recent years, praise for the U.S. management style increased as the U.S. economy improved relative to Japan. The executive officer selected by the Board of Directors represents the company and enters into an employment contract with the employees. In other words, a stock company (and the executive officer representing the company) serves as a nexus of various contracts such as an appointment contract with shareholders, employment contract with employees, lending contract with banks, and a sales contract with outside firms. This fact remains unchanged whether we consider Japan or the U.S. Since a company is a nexus of various contracts, both Japanese firms and U.S. firms "belong to shareholders" and "belong to employees".

A company in which the appointment contract is frequently changed and the employment contract is frequently changed because of the frequent change in the executive officer is called the "U.S. style". And, a company where such changes in appointment and employment contracts are difficult to make is called the "Japanese-style". In Japan, some say "governance by shareholders is unnecessary because governance by employees is functioning".

Different Models of the Stakeholder Firm

Germany and Japan share certain features as "stakeholder" models of corporate governance, while the U.S. style is for the more shareholder-oriented model of corporate governance. Some key similarities between the German and the Japanese systems include the following:

(1) Ownership stakes are held among shareholders having strong commitment to specific firms and focusing on their strategic interests.
(2) Banks play a central governance role and are the main providers of external finance to industry.
(3) Strong employee voice in corporate decision-making that supports the commitment as reflected in longer periods of employment and the lower sensitivity of employment to the business cycle.
(4) Management careers were largely internal to their firm, with less division of strategic and operational tasks.

Stakeholders display strong commitment and exercise voice rather than exit in order to promote the long-term survival of the firm. In the USA, management is more interested to promote the creation of shareholder-value.

There are some differences between the German and the Japanese systems (see Table 3):

(1) In Germany, ownership tends to be concentrated such as family ownership and vertically organized conglomerate holding companies (Konzern). By contrast, ownership within Japanese keiretsu groups is more diffused through horizontal cross-shareholding.

Table 3.   The different institutional foundations of stakeholder governance.

	Germany	Japan
Ownership	High concentration among stakeholders	Diffuse cross-shareholdings
Banks	Loans, shares, board representation, proxy voting	Loans, shares, occasional dispatched directors
Employee participation	Information, consultation, and codetermination rights	Usually information and consultation
	Legally mandated works councils and industry-wide unions	Enterprise unions
	Board representation	Informal interpersonal relationships with board
Wages	Flat age–wage profiles, linked to occupational qualification	Steep age–wage profiles
	Industry-wide collective bargaining	Enterprise-based bargaining
Skill formation	Public certification of training within tri-partite apprenticeship system	Firm internal training
Board of directors	Two-tier board with separation of supervisory and management functions	Single board, little separation of functions

Source: OECD reports.

(2) German universal banks are involved in lending, holding large blocks of shares, representation in the boardroom, and the exercise of proxy voting rights. Japanese main banks are linked to companies through lending and cross-shareholdings, but they play a lesser role on boards and proxy voting.

(3) In Germany, employee participation is vested in the institution of codetermination (*Mitbestimmung*) that specifies legal rights to information, consultation, and codetermination for work councils. In addition, employees hold between one-third and one-half of the seats on the corporate supervisory board, placing them alongside shareholders in appointing and monitoring management, giving business advice, and ratifying important strategic decisions. In Japan, participation rights are weaker and less formalized in law.

(4) In Germany, industrial relations are less centred on the individual firms. Industry-wide unions conclude uniform collective bargaining agreements with employer associations, making wages more similar across firms and linking them to occupation more than seniority. Training is similarly done in a standardized fashion according to publicly recognized occupational profiles. In Japan, collective bargaining, wages, and training are strongly enterprise-centred and reinforce the segmentation of firm-internal labour markets.

(5) Board of Directors in Germany follow a two-tier model where the supervisory and management roles are legally separated and strong rights are given to the supervisory board whose members include numerous people from outside the firm. In Japan, supervisory functions fall mainly to the statutory auditor, who lacks powers to appoint and dismiss management.

In Germany, the voice of labour and capital in the corporation is a matter of public interest and is supported through politics. In Japan, stakeholder voice is more closely dependent upon close mutual dependence within the firm.

Table 4 shows some performance measures of the 20 largest corporations in Germany, Britain, and Japan. Comparing Germany and Britain, the first group of indicators shows that shareholders in both countries receive a similarly competitive rate of return on their investment. Nonetheless, the second group of indicators shows that British corporations are valued much more highly in the stock market relative to their size. These differences in valuation are reflected in very different patterns of real economic activity, as shown in the third set of indicators: German firms occupy markets with lower profitability and employ over the twice the number of persons as their British counterparts. By contrast, Japanese corporations seem to be in a state of disequilibria, where high employment is combined with a medium level of capitalization to produce dismal shareholder returns.

While facing similar challenges, the different approaches to stakeholder governance in Germany and Japan have important consequences for how corporations respond to the challenges of international capital markets and shareholder pressure. German corporations have adopted

Table 4.   The performance of the 20 largest industrial corporations, selected averages (2000).

	Germany	Japan	United Kingdom
Returns to capital			
Price–earnings ratio	17.8	28.7	21.5
Dividend yield	2.7%	0.8%	2.6%
Return on equity	18.2%	5.7%	20.4%
Market valuation			
Ratio of market value to sales	0.51	0.97	2.14
Market value per employee	0.14	0.4	0.97
Price–book ratio	2.5	3.0	4.6
Sales, profits, employment			
Sales (mill. Euro)	38,122	44,579	22,015
Return on sales (EBIT to sales)	9.4%	14.4%	19.2%
Employees	138,072	147,581	60,676

Source: Own calculations based on Wrights Investors Information. Sample based on a ranking of sales in 1998.

a growing range of shareholder-value practices since the mid-1990s. Capital market pressures increased substantially, as witnessed by rising ownership by institutional and foreign investors, and the declining governance role of banks. German unions have given conditional support to shareholder-value measures but used their strong influence to "codetermine" the substance, to either improve managerial accountability or reduce class conflict by sharing gains with investors.

In Japan's enterprise community, similar institutional mechanisms outside the firm are developed to a much lesser extent. Markets are now discouraging the past dependencies between banks and industry. In the worst cases, corporate management is left increasingly unchecked (Jackson, 2003).

Sony's Corporate Governance

Sony is different from Honda regarding its corporate governance system. Sony adopted a "Company with Committees" corporate governance system, which is similar to the U.S. system. Sony has introduced the separation of the Directors' function from that of management and advancing the proper functioning of the statutory committees. Under this system, the Board of Directors defines the respective areas for which each Corporate Executive Officer is responsible and delegates to them decision-making authority to manage the business, thereby promoting the prompt and efficient management of Sony Group.

To strengthen its governance structure beyond legal requirements, Sony Corporation has added several provisions to its Charter of the Board of Directors to ensure the separation of the Board of Directors from the execution of business, and to advance the proper functioning of the statutory committees.

U.S. Sarbanes–Oxley Act and Governance Related to Disclosure in Sony

To comply with the established laws of the New York stock exchange, Sony has established a "Disclosure Controls and Procedures" system. It comprised officers and senior management of Sony Group who oversee investor relations, accounting, legal, corporate communications, finance, internal audit and human resources, advise the Chief Executive Officer (CEO), the president, and the CFO in the enhancement of the system and is responsible for the accuracy of financial reporting.

Sony Corporation applies its "generic strategy for competitive advantage and profitability in the electronics, gaming, entertainment, and financial services markets" (Meyer, 2017). An organization's generic competitive strategy establishes how the business competes against other firms. An intensive strategy specifies the approaches used to ensure business growth. As one of the biggest companies in the industry, Sony's case is an example of effective implementation of a generic strategy and intensive growth strategies appropriately developed, based on business needs and market conditions. Sony Corporation uses differentiation as its generic strategy for competitive advantage. Novelty and uniqueness were among the factors that led to the success of the PlayStation (Dess and Davis, 1984; Meyer, 2017).

Essence of Corporate Governance and Particular Characteristics of these Principles

In any organization, not limited just to companies, the executive managers must carry out their role of achieving the organization's objectives in a responsible manner. Corporate governance is a scheme for ensuring that the executive managers, who have been placed in charge of the company, fulfill their duties. The building of a logical and efficient corporate governance system is one of the main responsibilities of the shareholders.

It is believed that an interaction, characterized by some tension, between the executive manager with the highest degree of responsibility (the CEO) and the outside directors who have received their mandate from the shareholders, will lead to the practice of good governance. The CEO has the most responsibility for the management of the company.

The Board of Directors should supervise the management of the company by the CEO. The supervisory role of the board is premised on the fact that the decisions of the management team centred on the CEO will be evaluated by the securities market with the equity share market at its core.

Chapter 4

Quantitative Measures of Corporate Governance: A Critique

Introduction

The purpose of an effective corporate governance system is to create an effective organizational culture. A wealth of information exists in the relevant literature concerning the measurement of organizational culture (Hofstede, 1980, 1991, 1993, 1997; Cameron and Quinn, 1999; Denison *et al.*, 1995; Marcoulides and Heck, 1993; Kotter and Heskett, 1992; O'Reilly *et al.*, 1991). The purpose of this section is to analyze various studies on organizational culture, in order to identify the theoretical models of organizational culture and classify the measures of organizational culture. The structure of this paper consists of three major parts:

- identification of the theoretical models of organizational culture;
- overview of research on organizational culture;
- classification of the measurements of organizational culture.

Theoretical Models of Organizational Culture

In the last couple of decades, the concept of organizational culture became very important as it helps to understand and explain the most complex, irrational, and hidden aspects of an organization's life. Analysis of studies on organizational culture revealed the wide variety of ways of identification and interpretation of the concept of culture as well as variety of the organizational culture's dimensions. For example, Schein (1997) and Kotter and Heskett (1992) proposed cultural strength weakness as the main cultural dimensions, while Arnold and Capella (1985) identified a strong–weak dimension and internal–external focus dimension. Hofstede (1980, 1991) focused on power distance, uncertainty avoidance, individualism, masculinity, and Confucianism. Deal and Kennedy (1982) argued that degree-of-risk and speed-of-feedback are the main cultural dimensions. Kets de Vries and Miller (1986) proposed dysfunctional dimensions of the organizational culture including paranoid, avoidant, charismatic, bureaucratic, and pollicized dimensions. Cameron and Quinn (1999) identified four dimensions such as flexibility/discretion, stability/control, external focus/differentiation, and internal focus/integration which form four quadrants (clan, adhocracy, hierarchy, and market), each representing a distinct set of organizational culture types. Payne (2000) proposed a three-dimensional model of organizational culture: (1) pervasiveness (narrow–wide), (2) psychological intensity (strong–weak), and (3) strength of consensus (low–high). Schein develops the most comprehensive theoretical model of organizational culture based on the outcomes of the previous research on organizational culture. He combines, in the three-level model or organizational culture, the most important characteristics of organizational culture identified before such as espoused values (Deal and Kennedy, 1982), climate (Schneider, 1985), shared mental models (Hofstede, 1980, 1991; Van Maanen, 1979), shared meanings (Geertz, 1973; Smircich, 1983), shared symbols as ideas, feelings, and images, which groups develop sometimes unconsciously and also reflect the emotional responses of its members as contrasted with their cognitive responses (Hatch, 1990, 1997; Gagliardi, 1990) and, finally, organization's behavioural patterns (Trice and Beyer, 1985), organization's norms (Kilmann and Saxton, 1983), and organization's formal philosophy or mission (Ouchi, 1981; Pascale and Athos, 1981a, 1981b).

Schein's three-level model (1997) states that an organization's collective culture is based on shared basic assumptions such as unconscious emotional feelings, perceptions, and taken-for-granted beliefs, which are influencing espoused values like strategies, goals, philosophies, and subsequent patterns of behaviour of its employees, which form artefacts as visible organizational structures and processes.

Artifacts, behavioural patterns, espoused values all correspond to the conscious side of culture, while the basic assumptions which underpin a culture correspond to the ego in an individual's psyche. The unconscious side of the culture can be seen to consist of organizational specific constructs as well as national, religious, or racial–cultural constructs (Weber, 1930; Hofstede, 1980, 1991; Hofstede and Bond, 1988). Schein's definition of organizational culture as a collection of unconscious collective assumptions steering the values and, finally, through them, the artifacts and processes of the organization will be used as a working definition for current research; because this approach allows to try to understand why organizations behave in certain ways instead of just describing the differences in artefacts as some other studies do (Schein, 1997).

Overview of Studies on Organizational Culture

Organizational culture as a concept has a long history (Weber, 1930; Lewin, 1951; Likert, 1961; Laurence and Lorsch, 1967; Hofstede, 1980; 1991, 1997; Ouchi, 1981; Adler and Graham, 1989; Black, 1992; Denison and Mishra, 1995; Kirchmeyer and Cohen, 1992; Lubatkin *et al.*, 1997; Schein, 1997; Cameron and Quinn, 1999). Martin (1995) distinguished three traditions in the research on organizational culture: differentiation perspective, integration perspective, and fragmentation perspective. Having exposed conceptual differentiation, contemporary researchers must find some form of integration while researching the fragments of organizational culture; and only by taking into account all three perspectives, the researcher can understand and explain the dynamics of organizational culture better.

At the beginning, the concept of culture was used by anthropologists (Malinowski, 1961; Geertz, 1973; Kluckhohn and Strodtbeck, 1961; Kluckhohn, 1942, 1951) in the analysis of customs and rituals that nations developed during their history or the comparison analysis of values of Western and Eastern societies (Mead, 1949). Many of the recent studies (Schein, 1997; Hofstede, 1980, 1991) are derived from the works of anthropologists, and still use the ethnographic approach as way to describe as many facets of a particular organization as possible, similarly as it was done for a particular society. Even the term "culture" in organizational culture theory is bridging anthropologists' discoveries into organizational studies.

The next insight into a culture of organization can be found in classical works of Lewin (1951) and Likert (1961) who introduced the concept of organizational climate. Recently, many studies continue to use the concept of organizational climate along with concept of organizational culture and believe that those concepts represent different interpretations of the same phenomenon (Denison, 1984; Denison and Mishra, 1995; Marcoulides and Heck, 1993; Payne, 2000).

Organizational culture as research area was formed since the late 1970s and early 1980s concerning such aspects of organizational life as organizational symbolism (Gagliardi, 1990; Hatch, 1990), managerial symbolism (Schein, 1997), values (Kahle *et al.*, 1997; Cameron and Quinn, 1999; Zammuto *et al.*, 2000), and various sections of meanings such as leadership (Schein, 1997) and emotions in organizations. However, recently, most of the traditional constructs such as values, attitudes, emotions, and behavioural patterns are being reinterpreted and received slightly different meanings (Schein, 1997).

Aspect of Interrelationship between Organizational Culture and National Culture

Common for many researchers is the statement that organizational culture is forming under the significant influence of national culture (Weber, 1930; Mead, 1949; Geertz, 1973; Hofstede, 1991, 1997; Soutar *et al.*, 1999). Weber (1930) was one of the first researchers who stated the idea of a superior or "right" culture, which promotes economic growth and commercial success. Weber promoted "Protestant Religion" with its in-built rationalism as the proponent of economic success and he criticized Asian "Confucianism" for the backwardness of East Asia. However, recently, Hofstede (1993) has promoted "Confucianism" as the crucial dimension for economic success of the newly industrialized East Asian countries.

Thus, this debate is raising questions about the existence of the so-called "superior" culture. Schein (1997) pronounced that "assumption that there are better or worst cultures is superficial" and argues to avoid the superficial models of culture and builds on more comprehensive anthropological modes based on the identification and deciphering of the priority issues for members of an organization, leaders in particular. Culture is a system of shared values that serves two critical functions: (1) solutions of problems of external adaptations and (2) solutions of problems of internal integration (Schneider, 1985; Adler and Graham, 1989; Schein, 1997; Ralston *et al.*, 1997).

Hofstede (1980) argues the power distance measures the degree to which people accept the unequal distribution of power inside organizations. Uncertainty avoidance represents the degree to which people tolerate uncertainty and ambiguity in situations. Individualism as opposed to collectivism stands for the preference of people to belong to a loosely vs tightly knit social frameworks. Masculinity as opposed to femininity represents the degree to which people prefer values of success and competition to modesty and concern for others. The fifth dimension is called "long-term orientation", which captures the extent to which people have a future-oriented perspective rather than a focus on the present. Confucian dynamism illustrates this orientation (Hofstede and Bond, 1988; Kogut and Singh, 1988a). Cultural values and dimensions can be stable over time (Hofstede, 1980, 1991; Barkema and Vermeulen, 1997), but that is a debatable idea (Nordstrom, 1991; Adler, 1991).

Lawrence and Yeh (1995) have raised doubts about the originality of this fifth dimension, stating that the so-called "long-term orientation" is another version of "individualism". Kogut and Singh (1988b) along with Schneider and De Meyer (1991), Erramilli (1996), Barkema and Vermeulen (1997) have combined these five dimensions into one aggregate measure of cultural distance between countries, and found that the mode of foreign investment is influenced by the cultural distance between the home country of the multinational firm and the host country. This unidimensional index may cause oversimplification of the complex concept of cultural distance. For those multinational companies with joint ventures, cultural differences may create ambiguities and differences in relationship with the partners and subsidiaries, which may lead to conflict (Barkema *et al.*, 1996).

Various researchers have endorsed the popular concept of a "globalized" culture or "cultural convergence" (Ohmae, 1985; O'Reilly, 1989), and raised doubt about the meanings of Hofstede's five dimensions. Organizational change becomes very difficult where culture is well established in a successful organization. However, even a successful company has to modify its organizational culture, as cultural change is needed to adapt the organization to the changing circumstances of the business. If any culture fails to adapt to new conditions, it will be obsolete and can be the cause of the downfall of that organization (Kotter and Heskett, 1992).

A related argument is provided by the so-called "globalization" school (Levitt, 1983; Ohmae, 1985; O'Reilly, 1989; Friedman, 1994; Benerji and Sambharaya, 1996; Larsson and Finkelstein, 1999). According to those authors, multinational corporations are spreading a global culture, and along with it a specific type of universal organizational culture is emerging. That universal culture is the global extension of the western culture, which is homogenizing and threatening the obliteration of the world's rich cultural diversity. It is also a part of the Western domination of the fragile and vulnerable economies and cultures of the developing countries to maintain post-colonial dependent relationships, and the multinational corporations are at the forefront of that globalization process.

Recent movements by the World Trade Organization and other Western-dominated financial institutions to integrate world productions and to remove all obstructions to international trade and investments have intensified the globalization process. Due to Japan's economic stagnations since 1993, a number of major Japanese corporations (e.g., Nissan, Fuji Heavy Industry, Mazda) are now under effective Western control. A number of other corporations (e.g., Nippon Telephone and Telegraph) and some Japanese financial institutions have Western minority shareholders. As a result, Japanese organizational culture is changing and approaching the western organizational culture (Maruyama, 1961; Morishima, 1981).

Ouchi (1981) has discussed how a Japanese clan type of organizational culture can make an organization efficient. Similarly, Peters and Watermann (1982) along with Carroll (1983), Van de Ven (1983), and Kanter (1983) have demonstrated how companies with progressive human resource practices can improve their performance. These authors have tried to put forward a general theory of organizational culture and performance. Similar studies by Gordon (1985) and Kravetz (1988) have demonstrated that organizational cultures emphasizing creativity, autonomy, and participatory management can improve productivity. Calori and Sarnin (1991), in their study of the French management system, have shown that this link between organizational culture and performance is not restricted to any particular culture. What is true about the market-oriented system in the Anglo–Saxon culture or the clan-oriented system of Japanese culture is also true in the context of the social–market culture of continental Europe. Hansen and Wernerfelt (1989) have shown that internal organizational factors were stronger predictors of performance than market positions.

Bartlett and Ghosal (1989) consider the impact of differences between national characteristics. The greater the cultural distances, the greater will be difficulties for a multinational company to manage their foreign subsidiaries by themselves (Hennart and Larimo, 1998). When market transactions or contracts are subject to high transaction costs, sharing equity is efficient because it transforms input suppliers into co-owners in the venture. This would give rise to joint venture companies, which may have different organizational cultures.

Aspect of Interrelationship Between Organizational Culture and Corporate Performance

While the "national character" theory focuses on the national cultural characteristics, another line of arguments derived from the common belief is that organizational performance depends on organizational culture (Kotter and Heskett, 1992; Marcoulides and Heck, 1993; Denison, 1984; Denison *et al.*, 1995). Kotter and Heskett (1992) have put forward an analysis to evaluate the need for organizational culture changes and their relationships with performances of the company. A strong culture, by creating a high level of motivation among the employees can enhance the performance of an organization. Thus, if an organization has a strong culture in terms of effective beliefs, values, and behavioural patterns, the productivity of that organization would go up (Kotter and Heskett, 1992). In order to improve performance, it is important to develop a theory to identify variables that controls cultures and performances (Marcoulides and Heck, 1993). The result of cultural and organizational differences can be reflected in the criteria for evaluations of performances of a multinational company (Choi and Czechowicz, 1982; Borkowski, 1999).

Another common belief is that the most important factor in shaping organizational culture change toward the right direction is the leadership, without which no organization can implement culture change. The measurement of effective leadership, which can transform an organization, was debated in Bass and Avolio (1990), Schein (1997), and Tracey and Hinkin (1998).

Cameron and Quinn (1999) identified three types of leadership influencing the formation of organizational cultures in the multinational corporations: (a) parochial, (b) ethnocentric, and (c) synergistic. The first type occurs when the manager does not wish or cannot recognize organizational culture. Parochial-type managers believe that their way is the only way to manage. In the ethnocentric types of multinational organizations managers believe that their way is the best way to manage. They view all others ways as inferior. In synergistic organizations, managers believe that their way and others' way differ, but neither is inherently superior to the other. The first two types of management of organizational culture — ignoring and minimizing — occur naturally and are therefore quite common. The third type is when managers in multinational companies are able to recognize both the importance of organizational culture and its potential positive impact on company's performance and manage accordingly.

Thus, analysis of the relevant literature reveals that researchers tend to look at particular aspects of the organizational culture. Due to the evolving nature of the culture, there is no universal paradigm or theory about it. Our knowledge so far indicates that culture affects organizations in some fundamental levels. There are visible artifacts of organizational culture such as organizational structure, organizational processes, technology, rules of conduct, records, physical layout, and some behavioural patterns such as rituals. This is the socio–cultural system of the perceived functioning of formal organizational structures, strategy, policies, and management practices in the operational level of the organization. Under that system, we have organizational values and assumptions about the nature of organizational reality, which emerge from deeper understanding of often unobserved hidden feelings of the members of organizations. The "mythological" roles often played by leaders as ceremonial heads of organizations, teach organizational values and attempts to transmit organizational values (Reynolds, 1986; Cameron and Quinn, 1999).

Classification of the Measurements of Organizational Culture

The concept of organizational culture is mainly humanistic, beyond any scope of measurement in any direct way. Thus, organizational culture cannot be measured directly (Schein, 1997). However, the organizational culture's effects and manifestations can be evaluated by rating in some quantitative manners. In this chapter, we can demonstrate some attempts of the researchers in management to measure the impacts of organizational cultures and their manifestations on the effectiveness of organizations.

Recently, there are several attempts to measure culture which is apparently unmeasurable, through statistical inference and psychological perceptions and by constructing a system of interrelated structural equations. It is important to examine the link between organizational culture and performance, which can be studied formally by constructing a structural equation model (Jöreskog and Sörbom, 1993). The structural equation model will combine the main subjective and objective variables in the analysis of organizational culture. In this way, the model can explain the behaviour of the variables in terms of cultural dimensions. The theory and techniques of utilizing theories in improving organizations are not well developed yet (Mackenzie, 1991; Denison and Mishra, 1995).

Marcoulides and Heck (1993) have tried to incorporate the three levels of cultural influences by examining the effects of visible aspects of organizational culture with its hierarchical structure and technical complexity. These authors have put forward a structural equation model (Palich and Hom, 1992; Jöreskog and Sörbom, 1993) to assimilate all relevant visible aspects of organizational culture and performance in a model, to test some of the theoretical propositions regarding the interrelationships between culture and performance. Their model describes how organizational performance is affected by various exogenous and endogenous latent (unobserved) variables, and how these unobserved variables are related to the observed variables. This approach helps to understand the direction of causality and degree of relationship. The emerging paradigm of organizational culture depends upon specifications of certain parameters and traits of culture, which can be measured through the perceptions of managers and workers. These measures can be related to company performance, which can identify a set of parameters to understand the effects of organizational culture on effectiveness.

Another approach to measure organizational culture is based on evaluation of psychological characteristics of the managers (Myers and Briggs, 1962, 1980; Carlyn, 1977; Keen and Bronsema, 1981; Tzeng *et al.*, 1984; Schweiger, 1985). Meyers and Briggs (1962, 1986) developed the questionnaire "Myers–Briggs-Type Indicator", which can evaluate the psychological natures of the managers and may allow ascertaining what type of organizational culture a leader belongs to.

Cameron and Quinn (Quinn and Rohrbaugh, 1983; Cameron and Ettington, 1988, Cameron and Quinn, 1999), developed another method of measurement of organizational culture called "Competing Values Framework". Those authors designed a set of questionnaires to evaluate personality of the managers and, from these, the nature of the organizational culture they subscribed to. Usually, the set of questionnaires for survey, as the self-reporting system, incorporates some personal bias and, thus, this measurement tool evaluates only the upper layer of the organizational culture of the company under investigation rather than the core of corporate cultural assumptions. Cameron and Quinn (1999) have tried to avoid that problem by using geometric patterns of organizational cultures linking deep unconscious aspects of culture with its more tangible manifestations. The major advantages of this method is that the raw data obtained from these surveys can be manipulated by various statistical methods to evaluate relationships between the psychological natures of the managers and the natures of the organizational cultures.

Common approach to measure organizational culture is to contrast and compare the actual organizational culture and the ideal preferred one

(Cameron and Quinn, 1999; Ashforth, 1985; Brunsson, 1982; Day and Bedeian, 1991; Human and Berthon, 1991; Nutt, 1988). Once the raw data from the survey was obtained, researchers used statistical correlation analysis to estimate correlations between different types of managers and different types of organizations. Their results suggest that an ordered, effective culture would comprise a structured hierarchical organization with a strong goal focus. In contrast, the ordered participative culture would be a structured hierarchical organization where people were the centre of focus.

Organizations undergo changes as a result of mergers, acquisitions, and through deliberate changes undertaken by the management to make the organization more effective or to turnaround in the face of financial problem. In all these situations, culture can change. In the case of mergers and acquisitions, there are hopes that synergy created by the combinations of two or more organizations can uplift the culture. To measure the impacts of these changes in organizational culture, attempts were made by a number of researchers (Buono and Bowditch, 1989; Chatterjee, 1986).

Larsson and Finkelstein (1999) have combined a large number of such studies and studied the impacts of mergers and acquisitions on organizational culture and how it would change. Their approach is to create a large sample of 500 companies mentioned in the works of other researchers and combine the results of surveys made by various researchers to create large enough samples to examine the benefits and adverse effects of mergers on the organizational culture. After having the results of the survey which will reflect the opinions of managers and employees on the existing, changing, and expected organizational culture, co-relation analysis was used to determine links between various variables used in the description of organizational culture and effectiveness. Thereafter, a factor analysis was performed to determine the relative importance of the factors linking these variables. A structural equation model was employed to describe the relationships in a unified way and the validity of the structure was examined using standard statistical criteria. This study shows the applications of three techniques (correlation analysis, factor analysis, and structural equation modelling) to determine the nature of changes in the organizational culture after a merger or acquisition. However, the fundamental tool is the survey analysis on a sample of opinions of managers and others in different companies. Thus, sampling techniques is the core in this type of research as well.

Methods of Measurement of Organizational Culture

Most of scholars agree that the concept of organizational culture is very important in organizational theory; however, there are debates about the best methods to measure it. Traditionally, two large groups of scientists argue that only qualitative methods or quantitative methods are suitable to measure organizational culture. However, recently, the approach to combine both methods is very common (Denison and Mishra, 1995; Schein, 1997).

Schein (1997) proposed the Clinical Research Model to analyze organizational culture, where two scores: (a) level of researcher involvement (low/medium/high) and (b) level of subject involvement (minimal/partial/maximal) were used to combine quantitative methods such as demographics (measurement of "distral variables"), experimentation, questionnaires, total quality tools (statistical quality control); as well as different qualitative methods such as ethnography (participant observation, content analysis of myths, rituals, symbols, meanings), projective tests, interviews, and finally clinical (action) research of organization development.

Indeed, development of quantitative models should be based on extensive data from various qualitative methods such as historical event analysis, interview, focus groups followed up by surveys in order to understand precise nature of the functioning of culture and its influence on company's performance. Literature suggests that so far common approaches such as structural equation modelling and correlation analysis are at their exploratory stages regarding their application on the domain of organizational culture; further research to refine these quantitative models through imaginative applications will extend the existing knowledge on applicability of these methods as well (Marcoulides and Heck, 1993; Denison and Mishra, 1995).

O'Reilly has introduced the new instrument to measure organizational culture named Organizational culture Profile (OCP) and provided the summary of the literature regarding the common approach to use questionnaires in organizational culture measurement. They classify 18 instruments to measure organizational culture using survey methods published over an 18-year period from 1975 to 1992. The latest instrument to measure organizational culture named GLOBE was developed during large cross-national study of interrelationship of organizational culture and leadership (Dickinson *et al.*, 2000).

Comments

We have seen the efforts taken by various researchers to measure the nature of organizational culture. However, there is a serious problem of objectivity that exists in the area of organizational culture research as in any social sciences' area because of the inherent defects of the sampling methods and statistical inferences. Thus, measurement in social science is only an attempt to obtain some reflections of the truth. However, despite these defects, significant achievements have been made in recent years to design novel methods and models incorporating organizational cultures and their impacts on the company behaviour. Scholars have proposed a large variety of dimensions and attributes of organizational culture. The reason so many dimensions have been proposed is that organizational culture is extremely broad in scope. It implies a complex, interrelated, ambiguous set of factors. No one framework or measurement tool described so far seems to be comprehensive, nor one particular framework or measurement tool can be argued to be right while others are wrong. It is believed that the most appropriate framework and instrument to measure organizational culture should be based on empirical evidence and should be able to integrate most of the dimensions being proposed.

Chapter 5

Interviews with Executives
of Japanese Multinational Companies

In this chapter, we present some abstracts of interviews we have conducted with the most senior executives (president, vice-president, managing director, and plant directors of several Japanese companies (Toyota, Honda, Mitsubishi) in Japan, UK, Thailand, Australia, and India. In order not to identify their name and ranks, we provide below the transcripts of the interviews without indicating any names, or ranks, or companies.

Analysis of the Interviews

From the interviews, we obtained a picture regarding organizational culture as created by the corporate governance system of the major Japanese multinational companies (henceforth MNCs). We try to describe below what we have learned.

Japanese Management Practices and Principles

Japanese management model consists of two closely related systems: (a) the Japanese production system, commonly known as Toyota Production System (TPS), which was followed in every Japanese corporations and (b) the Japanese employment relations. The aim of Japanese MNCs is to transplant these systems to their subsidiaries abroad exactly, although it may not be possible always. The main features of the TPS is its flexibility, the capacity to adjust product lines in accordance with changing market demand, and the facility to change employee's inputs in accordance with changing production demands. In the management literature, this is described as "lean production" and "low-waste" system. There are three essential elements of the TPS: on-time delivery of reliable components; a system of quality control with zero defects for each component; and a production system with low cost automation, devices, and techniques that are labour-saving but inexpensive in terms of cost of capital. Central to these is a management system that emphasizes continuous improvement (*Kaizen*), regular consultation among the employee to improve quality and individual responsibility within a group for an employee with multiple skills with job rotations. Life-time employment, seniority-based wage system, and a company trade union subscribing to the value system and strategic goals of the organization. A subsidiary of Japanese MNCs in a foreign country always has these characteristics as these are in Japan. This signifies as very close relationship between the head office and subsidiaries of any Japanese MNC. It gives rises to a new model of MNCs that differs significantly from its Western counterparts. A high ratio of expatriate managers and the tendency of the subsidiary to leave much of the strategic and business decision-making in the hands of the head office are the characteristics that differ from their Western counterparts. However, there are variations.

Most subsidiaries implement the Japanese "just-in-time" inventory system within the plant, but the procurement from the outsider causes a serious deviation from the norms. Thus, transplantations of the Japanese inventory system in the subsidiary is not an objective, and subsidiaries have to adjust their production management practices according to the local conditions.

Japanese MNCs have long-term commitments towards both employees and the suppliers. Even during a crisis, as demonstrated during the Asian financial crisis in 1998, Japanese MNCs would not give up these commitments as far as possible. Less than 10% of the Japanese transplants in the Southeast Asian countries resorted to laying off regular employees. In Toyota, in Thailand, no regular employee was affected badly. The case was the same for local suppliers. However, this commitment depends on the global strategy of the headquarters but not on the business decision of the subsidiary. In the case of electronic industries in Europe, many Japanese companies withdrew their investments at the time of crisis.

The transfer of job participation system and wage system based on seniority can also be difficult. These are most successful in Korea and Taiwan, as both of them used to be Japanese colonies and thus are familiar to the Japanese management system. However, in Southeast Asia, employees do not have such an individual responsibility as they have in Japan regarding quality and maintenance of the production system. In USA, job classifications are reduced and are in line with the Japanese system at home. However, wages are not based on seniority and the vertical partition between jobs are high. This is due to the American wage system, which binds wages and job classifications.

In the UK, job classifications are now less, but there are still separations of skilled from the unskilled workers into different categories. In Europe, management representatives for each industry meet with union leadership each year to determine the basic wages for different types of job ranks. A company in a particular industry has obligations to follow its wage tables for the industry for the country or region in which the subsidiary is located. There is not much scope to implement the Japanese style of ranking employees on the basis of performance evaluations and the length of service. Thus, prior existence of management systems such as job-based wages and skill specializations in U.S. and Europe tends to create obstacles to implement the home management system from the head office in Japan in the subsidiary in Europe or USA. As a result of this, quality circles or *Kaizen* activities which are based on small group participations irrespective of job classifications are difficult to implement in Europe or USA. As a result, sharing of information across the vertical and horizontal classes of employees are difficult. That leads to in a subsidiary in USA or in Europe a non-participatory management system which is alien to the Japanese management system in the head office. Thus a subsidiary in USA or Europe may have a top-down approach of management, whereas in Japan a decentralized decision-making process is considered to be ideal.

To compensate for these deficiencies, Japanese MNCs have devised a number of methods. First, is the presence of Japanese expatriate personnel who would provide links between various classes of employees and coordinate activities with the head office more closely. The second element is the regular transfer of new technology from Japan to the foreign subsidiary to compensate for the lack of *Kaizen* activities. That enhances the authority of the head office on the subsidiary. The third element is to procure parts either from Japan or from the Japanese firms within the Keiretsu system located in the foreign country and not to rely upon foreign parts' suppliers, to compensate for the lack of proper quality control.

Interview 1: Honda-UK

Question (Q): It is about human factors, which influence performances; we want to examine whether organizational culture is the same in host and \home countries. It will be valuable to share your experience.

Answer (A): *Horensu* — do you know what it is? It is a very important discipline for Japanese organizational culture. It is a principal entry to the company. Most important discipline, if you visit Japanese companies, particularly the human resources department, you can find it written on the wall. It means Spinach. In Japanese organizational culture, we use it differently. It means — *Ho* for *Honkoku* or reporting, *Ren* means *Renraku* or to be influenced, and *Su* means *Sudan* or consult. Combination of these three words is *Horensu*.

Q: What do you mean by pre-consulting?

A: *Honkoku* is reporting. It is not difficult for Western managers to report. *Renraku* is also not strange. But, *Sudan* means any subordinate should pre-consult before he takes his own decision — even if the decision-making is within his power.

Q: With whom should he pre-consult — with the boss?

A: Decision should be taken before he makes his own decision.

Q: For work with minor decisions?

A: Boss is not interested in whether the things are minor or major; this pre-consulting is always required. For example, you can kill me, by telling me, "I have not heard of it".

Q: How do you do it? Officially or not?

A: It does not matter.

Q: So, before decision-making, you first consult, then you do. Do you think there is some slogan of the company — whether it determines the organizational culture of the company?

A: I do not think so; it is the company's objective.

Generally, top companies did not have any vision before. Now, it is a fashion to unite their employees. It has been a fashion for the last 10 years.

Q: So, is it not genuine Japanese culture? Is it not the Japanese way?

A: It is the opposite, to have objectives, annual objective, and so on.

Q: What is the Japanese approach then?

A: Japanese companies have used "slogan"; when you say slogan, for example, change the company for the fiscal year or reduction of quality control? Is it?

Q: If it is a mission, what is the purpose?

A: It is the western way, not the Japanese way. Japanese way is to enclose or unite the workers or members with some sense of equality; not the commercial company, but social companies, and membership of a society.

Q: Social welcome?

A: Special club or Unit.

Q: What kind of features are welcome?

A: Japanese companies have lifetime employment; freshmen entry is important, only they are the members.

Q: So, is it a society of Shinjins?

A: *Shinsotsu*, society of freshmen, after graduation from the university. To recruit only the freshmen.

Q: So, do they communicate among themselves?

A: Not communicate — human resources management has seniority system — but different from the American system. It consists of two parts, the wage system and the promotion system. Your question is related to the wage system. In the Japanese way, Japanese companies make groups by the entry year. All new recruits are from universities; for example, when I entered, I was in the group of 1965 entry group.

Q: How many groups are there?

A: One group per year. Length of service is important.

Q: Do you think still it dominates?

A: Yes. Very strongly.

Q: What kinds of people are welcome? Any particular features — like different personalities; what feature is popular in companies?

A: Every year, we research. We do research on the needs of the company and advise the students.

Q: Are they interested in qualification or human character?

A: Japanese companies do not pay attention to qualifications — human character is the most important.

Q: What kind of characteristics?

A: Positive to any assignments, flexible to any alternation of tasks, cooperation with colleagues — not disobedient, but cooperative. Do you know Japanese? This is about Japanese corporate system and human resources management system; you can find "freshmen to Japanese companies" — positive and cooperative.

Q: What do you mean by bright and intellectually bright?

A: Cheerful, optimistic — not intellectual; they do not care about the score.

Q: Who actually is tracing the students?

A: At present, there are two fields. The first one includes scientific works, engineers, chemists, etc. Japanese companies used to have connections with professors, who recommend students to the companies. Each company used to maintain these contacts.

The second is non-scientific — economics, law, and arts. In Japan, there is no such manner, each student personally applies — no connections with professors.

Q: How does human resources department recruit these managers?

A: No specific conditions, same as I have told you.

Q: Does the organizational culture affect the organizational performances — can you give examples from your company? We are trying to establish some case studies. This is our kind of abstract hypothesis — examples from real life.

A: In Japanese way of quality control, quality cycle — it is maintained under such a Japanese sense of consciousness; membership — employees work after the working time with no extra pay because it is important for the company. They sense, they are the members of the society, not just employees of the company. They don't feel subordinate workers like in western companies.

Q: It is called family type corporations? Is it?

A: It can be changed in future. Still it is very important. The time is passing, generations are changing — the new generation may adapt to the western type of young men.

Q: To be cooperative, optimistic, and collective — do you form these features in families or in the universities?

A: There are many explanations. One is from connections to the tradition of Confucius. I don't think so. It is the result of the system, lifetime employment, enterprise unions, seniority. Interest of the employee is the same as that of the company. It is the secret of the Japanese company.

Q: Is it because of some unwritten rule — from family in the under-conscious level — is it family?

A: Of course, disciplines at home, primary school, are important. But, I think the major reason is the system of Japanese corporation.

Q: So, this is the unique feature of organizational culture.

A: It is related to some cultural or historical matter. It remains because of the system.

So at the conscious level it is important when you start working. That is the reason why Japanese companies try to establish "*Horensu*". Not training, but discipline.

Q: You said, qualification does not matter. So, where does the training start for managerial works and how?

A: It may be only by entry year, by education, separate for high school graduates or university graduates.

Q: When do they separate them? How does this training take place?

A: In western sense, there is no special training.

Q: So, actually *Jinjibu* does this?

A: *Jinjibu–Hoski* — method. Western way is the boss system; each section has a manager responsible. In Japanese companies, it is carried by *Jinjibu* directly — to such cohorts by the entry year, not by line managers but by *Jinjibu* directly. Each year each boss can know only a few new freshmen under him. To maintain this knowledge to the whole of the new recruits for one year, *Jinjibu* is responsible — to keep the sheep as a Shepherd — everyone until the senior manager in the major Japanese corporations — it takes 15 years to become a section manager — *khacho*. This year, the 1985 group will be the section managers.

Q: How many people normally work for the *Jinjibu*?

A: Many more than in the western companies. It is very difficult in western companies for a human resources manager to become the CEO. In Japanese companies, they can become the CEO or the chairman of the board. So, the Western people would know nothing about the inner mechanism of the Japanese companies.

In western companies, managers may not participate in daily communications. In Japan, daily, they know all details through their bosses. When *Jinjibu* personally have direct interviews with the employees without their bosses, that is exceptional, normally it is through bosses. Collective training is held by the entry year, every 5 years and 10 years.

Q: What is the curriculum?

A: It can be diverse, even managerial. I have training in human resources management, and finance as in Western business schools; in Japan, the learning is from inside.

Q: Are there any examinations?

A: *Jinjibu* keeps the results secret, for the records used for selection for the promotions. Now, in Japanese companies, selection is made speedily.

I was in the first track; I became *Khacho* two years earlier than another group. Some others took some more time.

Q: The results of the training are thus very important?

A: Because Japanese companies do not need these at entry, there is no MBA system; freshmen simply means after university.

Q: Will it be successful to hire middle-aged people with better qualifications?

A: Only college graduates for management — there is no custom to hire graduate students. In scientific fields, it is different; graduate students, PhDs can be hired.

Q: Is there any training for engineers within the company?

A: My cohorts consist of scientists. We receive training on finance, HRM, etc. I learnt about Mintzberg in the company.

Q: Who are the lecturers?

A: In house — *Jinjibu* people teach HR, finance, and everything.

Q: What kind of qualifications do they have?

A: Same as others. Sometimes, *Jinjibu* invite professors as part-time lecturers.

Q: Did it happen in your case?

A: Some special lectures on how Japanese society is changing — seminars — some company presidents of another company taught us top management thoughts.

Q: What was the approach of your company to measure performances?

A: In Japanese companies, they do not use such things. They have market share, return ratio on sales; ROE, ROA are related to these. Many Japanese companies now mention these.

Q: So, it is changing?

A: Apparently — I am not sure whether it is real or not.

Q: Who determines the corporate culture?

A: Difficult to answer.

Q: May be in terms of your own company.

A: To change anything is the most difficult thing for Japanese companies. Because no Japanese businessmen have MBA and all are trained inhouse, they are not trained to certain levels to implement the western way of decision-making. So, Japanese companies change when company figures become red.

Q: You determine linkages go from top to bottom — is it so? — top managers determine organizational change or it is consulted from below?

A: Generally, it is based on *Horensu*, as long as the company is doing well. But if the company has to change because of compulsions, then top–down approach may be applicable. There are two ways — top-down and bottom-up.

Q: Can we say bottom-up is *Horensu*?

A: No, bottom-up is only direction; *Horensu* is the method of decision-making. Bottom–up or *Ringi* system in Japanese is the formal way of decision-making. When one has to propose something, he has to circulate his proposal to the related section like new training system or budgeting — before it will go to the boss.

Q: Next stage is to inform the boss?

A: Yes.

Q: Another question — what kind of organizational culture occurs in Japanese MNCs — whether it is the same or there is a change for the last 25 years?

A: Many people say such formal changes can be very rapid. Informal changes take time.

A: Can you recall formal changes in your company?

A: It did not happen in the last 25 years, only very recently — like the new reward system replacing the seniority-based system and the new wage system.

Q: Is it copying the western wage system?

A: They said, it is a hybrid system of Japanese and Western, i.e., how to do things in the *Jinjibu* way. *Jinjibu* staffs once prepared materials to persuade a worker with bad behaviours to change ways; but when one American submanager said, why not fire that guy, the *Jinjibu* could not answer.

Q: So, *Jinjibu* was trying to train local managers in the Japanese way — but this is not always a success.

A: Formal part is not a problem, it is the same everywhere. Informal parts are difficult.

Q: Inner mechanism is different. Thank you very much for your time — there will be some questions in the survey I like to conduct, but you can do it afterwards.

A: Thank you.

Interview 2: Mitsubishi-Thailand

Q: We are studying major aspects of organizational culture and its relationship to performance. We like to ask you some questions regarding corporate governance and operations in Mitsubishi.

A: MMC was established in the 1970s, so it is a new company. Its organizational culture is derived from the Mitsubishi heavy industry. In Thailand, we are here for about 20 years.

Q: Is there any style of doing things in your company? Any example, like slogan or mission of the company. It is a great opportunity to ask the top manager of such a large Japanese corporation, what they think about it.

A: Continuous growth and economic development — these are the missions of our company.

Q: Is it changing over the last 20 years since it was established?

A: Sales growth, market share increase and efficiency, and continuous growth are still the mission. In past, the company used to depend on traditional behaviour such as the Japanese style of lifetime employment, seniority, keiretsu system, Japanese industrial policy, relationship between private and government, and assets like real estate. Now, market valuation means much for profit. These have changed. Mitsubishi Group is available for all the companies in the group, especially for MMC which used to enjoy these characteristics — not very much at present — Daimler-Chrysler characteristics are changing because of these — it will reflect on our vision and style taken by our company. In the past, the company used to focus on many products, now the focus is on the customer.

Q: After the acquisition by Daimler, do you think the culture of Daimler influences the MMC now?

A: It was just introduced very recently; there is not much change now. It was not successful. No, we do not take much from them — here, not at all.

Q: I like to know whether the individualistic approach of the western companies will be introduced in MMC in future?

A: Top managers normally introduce new cultural changes. Three board members are from Daimler — not so much changes in the manufacturing style, but, in the board, there will be some changes; that means there will be influences on managers.

Q: Does Japanese national culture have any influence on the organizational culture of the MMC?

A: Thirty years have passed. Manager's background and organizational culture does not depend so much on Mitsubishi Heavy Industry, which comes from 1857 and is connected to the national culture. MMC is different. Members from Daimler are appointed at the level of board manager and top manager. So, everything is changing.

Q: So, the people in MMC are more cosmopolitan, and it does not support national culture anymore?

A: Regarding changes among people, basic structures of the national culture has not changed, but some techniques of the management has changed. National culture has changed in 30 years, but a long time is needed to make impact on the companies. Now, there are also international students.

Q: People from other countries are influencing Japanese culture, is it? Do top managers believe national culture can increase the performances of the company?

A: Among these situations of the domestic market, national culture can get affected, but it is now a global economy, so there may not be much intensive relationship in the global market. Within Japan, national culture and organizational culture are combined, to be supported in the domestic market management. In global management, such a situation will change.

Q: I like to know whether the MMC in Japan is different from the MMC in Australia? Are they different culturally or is the organizational culture homogeneous all over?

A: Not so much difference in the management; top managers are Australian, and some Japanese work together with them. Organizational culture is not different.

Q: Is it required to transfer similar features from Japan to Australia?

A: Most of the capital is from Japan, not much changes regarding culture of the company.

Q: In your opinion, who determines the culture of the company in Japan?

A: Slogan is "good product". Now, the aim is to create good sales and everything has become customer-oriented. The relationship between the company and customers will continue. So, once the policy is decided by the board members, all workers and managers work on realizing the policy. Such a process gives rise to the organizational culture, and the organizational culture is thus formed through this process.

Q: So, the company policy comes from the top level?.

A: In director's meetings, board members decide about policy.

Q: If the lower managers try to suggest improvement, is it welcome?

A: They suggest and we welcome.

Q: Do you call it *Kaizen*?

A: Yes.

Q: How does it happen? How do you welcome? How do you implement it?

A: It is not only through the workers; managers and engineers must support these.

Q: Is there any system of awards? How?

A: Suppose 10 workers are in a unit, if eight persons do the same, and two persons will do the same. This plan is a contribution — it denotes some monetary or technical advice which they jointly complete.

Q: Is it honourable? Is there any psychological support? The pictures of these workers are hanging in the office, etc. or are there some honourable rewards?

A: Our personnel division will evaluate these.

Q: Is it possible that your division will evaluate these?

A: In manufacturing, yes. The role of the manager is important. They cover various aspects of the plants, management of manufacturing, and so on.

Q: What is your personal opinion on whether national culture affects organizational culture in USA or Australia?

A: Organizational culture is concerned with the local company, so it does affect. In Japanese companies, it does not change according to the national culture — it changes from Japan to Thailand, for example. It varies from country to country; it depends on the capital structure to some extent. It is extremely difficult to exclude the local culture from management, so the management will adopt the local national culture.

Q: Is there any difference, say, MMC in USA and MMC in Australia regarding the effects of culture?

A: U.S. management is changeable, in a sense, many techniques are being developed. Australian culture is from the UK, some differences are there in management techniques. Australian operations are not so profitable because of the high taxation. It is not so clear whether this will continue in future, due to high tax operations.

Q: Which domestic culture affect the organizational culture strongly, Australian or American?

A: The managers of MMC carry with them to the Australian and U.S. operations, techniques of management and manufacturing, but not much of the Japanese national culture. Personnel management, promotion, etc. are according to the local culture, but manufacturing is as per the Japanese system.

Q: Is it possible to do a survey, of about 20 questions, from the managers of MMC.

A: Yes, it is possible. But I think the head office's senior managers' opinion can be similar in most cases.

Q: Thank you so much for your help.

Interview 3: Toyota-Britain

Q: I have some questions to lead the conversation. It is very valuable for us. We try to connect performance to human factors. It is very difficult to find out information, to find out what it means by Japanese corporation. Is there any style of doing things? We will keep everything very confidential.

A: Japanese way of doing business — one of the typical way is — important matters will be decided not by managers, but by meetings of managers. If we have problems, we have a meeting. If it is a minor issue, it will be solved by assistant managers' meetings, if it is important, then senior managers' meetings will be held.

Q: How many people are responsible for decision-making?

A: It can be 20, it can be 30. If a company is going to buy another, it will be decided by the Board of Directors, not by the president or vice-presidents. In minor matters like buying stationaries, the junior managers will decide.

Q: Do you need meetings to buy stationary?

A: It depends on the importance of the matter. Usually those who are most interested call for the meeting. All members will make suggestions, and the final conclusion will be made. If it is small, it is oral; if it is important, then written.

Q: Who is responsible for hiring people?

A: Most companies have personnel department (*Jinjibu*). How to decide depends on which level of employees you are talking about.

Q: Suppose, middle managers.

A: All managers are hired just from college. They are promoted gradually.

Q: There is a hierarchical method of training. What happened next?

A: It depends on companies. Normally new recruits will be coached on the basic matter for one month, then transferred to a branch for 2–3 months, then they will be assigned to certain departments. Usually, someone will be appointed as the in charge of new recruits and day-to-day business transaction training. All of them go out to meet new customers and to discuss business. New recruits are allowed to take notes.

Q: For himself?

A: For company records. After 2–3 years, when the training period is over, he will be assigned with certain customers. After some years, he will have subordinates who are to be trained to do their own work. There are many many ranks of managerial positions.

Q: What are the names?

A: New recruits are called *Shinzin*.

Q: When he gets subordinates, then what do you call him?

Q: *Shinjin* is the name and he has the lowest rank in office; actually, he is not the manager and he is managing himself. There are the associate managers or assistant managers (*Fukucho* or *Fukukacho* or *Gicho* or *Khancho* or *Khacho dairai*), then there is the deputy Manager (*Ku Khacho*), and then the section manager (*Khacho*).

A: It is very interesting to see how the new trainee grows up.

A: *Khacho* is the first stage. Next stage is the assistant general manager (*Bucho Dairai*), then there is the deputy general manager (*Kubucho*), and the general manager (*Bucho*). In some companies, *Kubucho* is higher than *Bucho Dairai*. It is now changing; previously, *Kubucho* used to be higher than *Bucho Dairai*. In between there is another rank, *Gicho*.

Q: We see sometimes *Kakaricho*.

A: That is before *Kacho*. Sometimes *Kakaricho* is the preliminary manager. This used to exist 40–60 years ago, but not now.

Q: During decision-making, for small issues, is any particular individual responsible? Or, is every member of the committee responsible?

A: For small matters, *Kakaricho* or *Kakacho* is answerable.

Q: For hiring, who is responsible?

A: General manager of the personnel department. Meetings will decide this.

Q: What are the influences of people outside *Jinjibu*? Any features or characteristics for promotions?

A: *Jinjibu* is main, but other departments can recommend. Regarding promotions, no one can decide except personnel department.

Q: Is it possible to tell us a particular slogan of the company? Does it determine the organizational culture of the company?

A: Most have slogans. It is always slogan; it is displayed or explained in magazines. Actual business is not influenced by it. It is a shame, not to have a slogan. Usually, they ask the consulting firm to make a slogan. Directors may explain to the employees about the business in their own way.

Q: What is meant by the power unite members of the company?

A: Unwritten slogans, which can be dictated by every member. The company does not advise usually. Employees can have common sense — what you should do or not.

Q: Give some examples, rules of doing things, just examples.

A: Unconscious remarks, very difficult. We think money — we have what is not company's money; it belongs to the shareholders. The company's money is collected from many. We should not use the money indiscriminately, but for the use of those activities which we are entitled to receive.

Q: Is it the usual behaviour of national characteristic?

A: For all the employees there are unwritten rules and also something else that determines the manners of the company — these are the features of organizational culture.

Q: What kind of behaviour is good behaviour?

A: Anyone can suggest something good, but insistence on one's own opinion is not good. It is good to suggest something. But if he continues to insist, then he will be considered to be non-cooperative Even it is a good opinion, if others are against it, he should follow the majority decision — otherwise, he will be excluded unconsciously from the group and eventually expelled from the company. Cooperation is the most important factor to remain in the company.

Q: What else?

A: Patience. You will not be short tempered; if your opinion is declined even for once or twice, you should not instantly say good-bye, but stay instead. In the company, every 3–4 years, the managers or subordinates change, and if you cannot endure new people you will be transferred.

Q: What else?

A: Obedience.

Q: From different aspects, is it good to be open-minded or you have to be shy?

A: Openness is welcomed. If you will be too open, you can have enemies.

Q: Why? Enemies?

A: Open mindedness means disclosing bad things too. If you say someone is not good, eventually the person will hear.

Q: Is there anything — like some kind of set features (*Jinjibu*) used to promote — psychological testing? Or, something *Jinjibu* expects to do?

A: We used to have, but now we do not use. Instead, they will ask many persons to do the interview. In part, only *Jinjibu* will interview. Now, production manager and finance manager also interview. They are doing tests, psychological, but not written.

Q: Did you have some experience?

A: I myself had.

Q: What are the set of psychological features for a good employee? Some kind of unit of characteristics?

A: Let me explain. When *Jinjibu* himself was recruited, it was by means of written tests. Those who can study very hard can pass examinations. Suppose, all are good in study but cannot do business — that is the reason the policy has changed — and all other managers interview. Final decision will be made by *Jinjibu*, from those who are hired, check the first, then others, they try to find an appropriate way, they ask old employees to recruit new graduates. I was too old to be assigned for that job.

Q: Our research is how organizational culture influences organizational performance. Do you think it really happens in real life? Can organizational culture increase productivity?

A: Difficult. Every company has a different culture — some do business well, some bad. There is no proof that this is bad or good for production or success. Every factor is mixed up; not only the culture, the financial technical ability also combines, which makes the company successful. It is true that the organizational culture affects the result. Every company will and must try to find out which culture was successful.

Q: This is what they are trying to do — to find out. In the beginning, it is preliminary to see what happens in real life. Can you tell us about OC, can it be formed by national culture? Or is organizational culture independent?

A: I think national culture affects organizational culture, basically.

Q: Being Japanese means managing in the Japanese way.

A: Collective decision-making process; cooperation is the most important factor for the employee. Seniority-based promotion.

Q: What about the approach — insider/outsider — you belong to the group or out?

A: Japanese employees think they belong to a certain company that resembles a family. We should not quarrel with each other but cooperate. Do job as effectively as possible. Corporation is a family — Japanese way of thinking.

Q: Family approach has changed or not? Recently?

A: I think it is changing, but still basically they think in that way, they will retain employees as much as possible. In recent years, they have to cut employment to survive.

Q: Does it affect organizational culture?

A: It is against the Japanese organizational culture, but it has to be. Most companies are reducing the number of people.

Q: Organizational culture can be transferred from host to home or home to host?

A: It depends on the local staffs. If the local people are more, the local culture will be strong. Otherwise, the Japanese culture will prevail.

Q: Who determines the corporate culture?

A: Everyone.

Q: Everyone or top managers?

A: Top managers cannot determine. They can have a slogan, but it is only a slogan.

Q: But they can downsize.

A: Most of the important matters have to be decided by the meeting.

Q: Collective opinion?

A: Yes.

Q: How does it work?

A: Someone who is most interested will ask to gather to talk; if all members of the board decide you have to wait until one month. If the meeting is to be held, those who promote will explain first about the concept. Discussion will then be about going for or against the plan. Sometimes, those who are for the plan can influence those who are against it and *vice versa*. So, the meeting will be held in this way.

Q: How does the debate happen?

A: Usually it is quiet. Every director has a line of responsibility. He will not interfere with the directors. These people will be silent. So you have to meet everyone personally and explain and pursue to favour the proposal.

Q: You already arrange the opinion — what is required for foreign employees?

A: There were no directions for foreign employees, for subsidiaries, there are some non-Japanese directors. In that case, in British subsidiaries, they do not have vital interest in the management of the company; Japanese directors plan all and circulate the plan to others. I have not experienced heated discussions.

Q: How do you measure performance?

A: It used to be more premium volume, more volume means more profit. Now, volume does not mean big profit and net profit is important. It used to be equal profit based on sales volume, but not now.

Q: You who have spent 32 years with this company. Do you think organizational culture has changed?

A Small changes, but basically the same.

Q: What has changed for good or worse?

A: Seniority rules are changing. Even if young, the eligible can be promoted quicker than others. It used to be the case when you join at the age of 22, you become assistant manager at 32, manager after 39, and almost all promotions were in that order. Now, someone who is sick cannot be promoted as the manager. Before, it was different, and it is changing now. The company now hires middle-aged employees. Fifty years ago, it was impossible and it was not the case. But, it is basically the same culture.

Q: *Kaizen*, do you have this in your company?

A: *Kaikaku* — rapid changes, *Kaizen* — continuous improvement; yes, we have this in our company.

Q: We have covered all, and we need your permission to do some other survey, if you have the time. Thank you for your time, we have gathered a lot of information.

Interview 4: Toyota-India

Q: Let me say that the corporate philosophy consists of different people — top managers. We are doing research on the effects of national culture on corporate culture and performances. I have been to Britain recently, and now I am in India.

A: In Britain, we have production base in Derby and corporate office in London. I have visited Britain only two weeks ago. In India, we have started production recently.

Q: We have a major question — is there any particular way of doing things — any style or slogan or mission?

A: We are keeping the basic philosophy for many years — TPS. It is out symbol — philosophy. It is becoming very famous. We had very difficult time with labour unions in 1950s in Japan. We had sad experiences. After that, we had strong cooperation between management and union, and we are maintaining good relations. We believe, it is very important to motivate for the company. We are introducing, in Japanese, *Soyokoku*; employees are always welcome to make a proposal to improve any kind of job. We receive a lot of proposals. Constantly, we stimulate the activity.

Q: How do you motivate?

A: We make some allowances, payments are based on awards on proposals, and it is open to all, a relaxed atmosphere.

Q: It is very honourable to get the awards, I think.

A: Yes, it depends on how many proposals they can make per year. This activity is effective to motivate people. We get good proposals to improve productivity and safety. We have introduced this in our overseas bases in both production and clerical works.

Q: Any proposals for improvements are welcome, I think.

A: It is based on their actual job. Not necessarily job-related. *Kaizen* — we call it continuous improvements — never stop — in any area of our business, especially production.

Q: Is this approach very traditional Japanese or special to Toyota?

A: In Japan, the relationship between managers and employees is very close compared to the Western countries. In Western countries, there are clear separations between management and employees. In Australia, it is very strong — very clear differentiation — many conflicts. In India, it is between Australia and Japan. In Japan, it is not the case. In some companies in Japan, controlled by the Communist Party, there were very demanding unions. To make companies profitable, we have contributed to the future happiness of the employees, after the 1950s conflicts.

Q: How do you create a friendly relationship? Do you have workplace meetings?

A: Yes, we have periodic meetings. Between managers and union.

Q: In your opinion; does national culture influence organizational culture?

A: Japanese national culture influences our organization — Japanese people put values on "harmonization". We do not like conflicts. We do not loudly claim our personal demands. We put values on our social groups — happiness — this exists for many years — we do not like conflicts. In USA, lawsuits are very common — lots of lawyers — too many — the cause is not specific. In Japan, people do not like that.

Q: Is it due to difference in legal system? Can you harmonize other characteristics of national culture?

A: Many years ago, Japan was broken completely. We started from zero; we are very poor in natural resources. The only way the economy succeeded was exports to buy natural resources. After World War two, every Japanese worked very hard to make better life, in that period, many companies improved rapidly to make everyone happy. Working hard means naturally strong good results and career expansions — continuous expansion. We were very happy up to 10 years ago; then Japan went into a different stage.

It was very easy before to have a job target, to be stronger, to compete, and to export. The target was very simple for everyone. During these last 10 years, this was very difficult.

This philosophy is very clear; hard work to get better life, quite understandable for everyone, this the national culture — a unique situation.

Q: Does historical situation form natural characteristics?

A: Specially after 1990, situation changed very speedily — ours of course, but this was true for entire Japan. We cannot continue the past procedures. The past methodology has to change in many areas; it is not easy to change the company culture too quickly. Our task was to change in order to meet the new environment. We have faced the appreciation of Yen many times. Before 1971, Yen was 360 per $, after that it became 120 Yen per $ in 30 years. Situation like these — sudden appreciations — cause trouble because Toyota is an export company. Often, we face financial difficulty, but we have enough energy to overcome. We set targets, everyone works hard to achieve the target. We have faced that type of challenge — in 1993, two or three times, we did. We call it a kind of devil cycle. We challenge very hard, we overcome, again and again, endless cycle. We call these last 10 years as the lost decade for Japanese companies, as the economy was losing power and the so-called "right hand shoulder rising" trend completely changed. At the same time, the economy is becoming borderless, progress in IT developments means globe becomes narrow. The picture is different; global information exchange is taking place. Previously also there was competition, but now it is nearly global.

New challenge is the environmental issue. If automobile industry wants to expand in future, environmental issue is essential. We may have dramatic changes in technology. We survive in the 21st century. We put large resources to develop future technology. Now we have global automobiles industry. We have developed fuel cell; it is a key for automobile industry. Future will have dramatic changes and our purchasing behaviours change because of Internet. The distribution channel is very old-fashioned; we may have dramatic changes in the distribution organization.

Q: Does that mean, customers' matters can dictate changes in your organizational culture?

A: Yes, distribution is old and outdated.

Q: What is your vision of new challenge?

A: We understand the problem. Only Toyota has five different sales channels, each one is a different model. In some cases, two sales networks handle one product. Some customers go to dealers who may not handle the products. That type of inconvenience is there in our current system. Of course, Toyota has various models, customers want to compare the model with other products like Nissan or Honda. Currently Nissan is minimizing their networks; the customer distribution system is not convenient. In USA, you have malls, in Japan there are few, but this problem will not last long. They may select other methods we have to modify, but it is very difficult as lots of dealers do not want to change.

Q: Are the expectations of the organizational culture for dealers the same?

A: We are basically having contract with each other. Dealers are not subsidiaries; they are handing 100% of Toyota products except finance, and they want to keep their rights. From the technological point of view, drastic changes are required, distribution sales also needs to be changed, we cannot expect customer's growth in future. Employee policy has to be changed. Lifetime employment was the best policy — salary based on age and experience — but it does not work anymore.

We cannot expect continuous growth anymore. Employment policy is changing drastically.

Q: Any example?

A: We started changes in the salaries for managers. In the past, within a rank, we had different salaries based on experiences. About five weeks ago we have changed — now, we have same salaries regardless of experiences. In many cases, the age of the people in a position was important. New freshman's salary was much lower than someone in the same rank with many years' experiences. In the new system, we have same salaries, but performances determine the actual salaries which will be different.

Q: What are the criteria of performances?

A: Before starting their yearly career, they declare their mission statement. They evaluate their performances first by themselves. After that the manager evaluates, then *Joshi*, one rank above managers, evaluates them. Actually, there are three revaluations.

Q: Is evaluation by Joshi the final?

A: Usually, the final evaluation depends on *Joshi* who are two ranks above the person.

Q: Would he get promotion then?

A: He needs to perform well continuously for 2–3 years, and then he will be promoted to a higher rank. A single year is not enough.

Q: Who creates the first mission?

A: We have an organizational mission, starting from the target of the company. It can be broken down into some set of narrow responsibility to show what the missions of individuals should have. After that, they develop tasks based on the company's mission.

Q: Is this the organizational culture?

A: They create individual missions — discuss it with *Joshis* — everybody actually. But this is not applied for the workers; only for the salaried managers. For workers we do not use this system. We have to change this type of personnel policy. We are now shifting to the American method. In Australia, lifetime employment and salaries based on age are not popular. In the past we have maintained that — now we are changing. But still the "lifetime employment" is useful for keeping loyalty.

Q: So, you have a family type of organization, but it is changing — yes or no?

A: Yes, yes; it is changing.

Q: How do you measure loyalty?

A: It depends on daily working attitudes — it is very difficult to measure — *Joshi* always pay attention to that.

Q: Is there a reporting system with *Joshi* reporting to the upper level?

A: Yes, it is based on the mission — finally, appraisal by clear number, scores — how much scores — based on that score we have final ranking. Every employee has their own scores — A/B/C/D/S — ranking based on performances.

Q: What is S?

A: S — it is very difficult to make individual scoring; relative scoring is possible. Top 5% are S — very small class of top managers — majority will be B. The worse side D is not very usual. The actual salary is based on that ranking. This is not on mission statement. It is difficult to keep the past method — it meant to change to the Western method to keep better loyalty — it is not too popular to change company rules quickly. The difference between USA and Japan is the acceptance of enterprise culture. There is a lot of energy in USA — in college students, in people like Bill Gates, and there are lots of sponsors and financial support to take risks. But, in Japan, no, it is difficult.

Q: How do you measure performance of your company? Our research is about organizational performances — what is your approach?

A: There is some global market share ranking in the automobile industry. Currently we are not market leader, sometimes we fell. GM can be the No.1; we will continue to catch up with Ford and finally GM. Why Toyota wants to expand? Our product is much superior, in environment, Toyota's role will continue, we are not expanding our business without that type of philosophy. Key word is to harmonize growth. In 1995, we set Toyota's 2005 vision — stakeholder, shareholders, society, employee, customers, need to harmonize growth — that is the symbol. Second is profit — essential for investment. In Japan, ROA/ROC concepts are not important — shareholders were silent — we did not put importance on ROA/ROC. This is another area we are having drastic change. We are now listed in NY/London — we start to pay more attention to ROC/ROA. In the past, we put importance on own capital — market share, profit, sales volume, production; these were important in Japan, as major performance indices.

Q: Our hypothesis is that organizational culture influences organizational performance. What do you think about it? In Toyota does it have positive influences?

A: I think so; Toyota is located in the country area, Nissan is located in city area, and they are individualistic. Here people think about the company. Once the company shows the direction, it is easy to gather the rest — we call in Japan "*Jensai Ichigan*" — all is one — very easy to go in one direction. We have that type of culture — Nissan people have individualistic performance — they are not so simple. We here have the kind of power to gather to "Kusinroku" centre, once we decide the target; we gather together. That type of organizational culture is very common for us.

Q: What is the major trait or characteristics of your company's organization — for example, loyalty. Something like this?

A: You mean organizational culture in Toyota — I will put dedication, consistency, adaptability, mission — in that ranking. It is a very easy organization to gather together.

Q: No data like that exist anywhere. We learnt a lot from you — no one in the academic world knows the changing directions of Toyota.

A: The challenge is whether we can; we have to keep the past culture and change.

Q: We ask what the preferred culture is, and we compare with the existing culture. What do you think?

A: It is very difficult to change culture. We did a good job — had success in the past — so it is very difficult to change. In our case, CEOs are giving message to the managers that it is necessary to change — otherwise we cannot survive — we are repeatedly giving messages to our managers' class; we are changing our direction.

Q: Can we ask your permission to do the survey among your managers in order to do the research we need? Is it possible to do the survey to distribute the questionnaire?

A: How many samples do you want to have?

Q: 200 at least, is it possible? There are 18,000 employees, 1,000 are managers, and this is my idea.

A: I am now responsible for the overseas operations. I have to get in touch with some directors who are in the personnel.

Q: Any number like 200 is Ok.

A: Ok.

Interview 5: Honda-Thailand

Q: Actually my research is about corporate culture and corporate performance, their relationships with national culture. Whether there is a link between corporate culture and performances? We stick with high performance Japanese MNCs. Our hypothesis is, corporate culture is related to the national culture. The first question is whether there is a link between national culture and corporate culture.

A: I have worked for the company for 20 years — it has joint venture with foreign companies. Under this background I will respond to your question. Your question is related to the historical background and international environments. Traditional Japanese national culture has undergone transformation to a global direction. It is changing, you cannot tell for sure what would be in tomorrow, and it is going through drastic changes due to technological transformations. When I started, everything was managed under the Japanese system. Since 1990 it is changing to the American-influenced system.

Q: Do you think national culture, because of drastic technological change, is changing as well? Do you have some examples?

A: In the computer communication, technology was originally invented by Bell in 1876; computers came after the world war, in 1946. The technology was different. It was analogue; now, it is digital. In 1947, transistor was invented. Technology was merged. Business has changed from traditional to international. That also influenced the internal organization.

Q: You mention Japanese way of doing things. What are these?

A: Decision-making function of each person — each person used to make some of his decisions when I have first started, and it used to take a long time to do any correspondence from the person to the manager. As result of the computer technology, now we can get the draft from one side to another without the approval of the manager.

Q: There is system — *Horensu* — does it exists in your company? Do you still have?

A: It is not so recognized as Japanese. It is a way to keep good communication. There are so many modes — important matter, routine matter, and strategic matter; we cannot simplify. In general, the trend was to be controlled by the management. Today every facet has become responsive and responds in a short time.

Q: Japanese approach — consult the boss, approval with manager — does it exist?

A: It is the same thing. One of my job was licensing of patent, know-how. In case of other people approving the license, internal discussion with the division in which patent is involved has to be carried out. The profit centre division should also be consulted to receive and grant the license. The supporting division may have an interest in consulting with the legal division. Apart from these, units like the patent division and financial section should be consulted. Sometimes, foreign countries should also be involved.

Q: Can you recall about the features of corporate culture that are most important?

A: Most important culture is to achieve customer satisfaction — this is the most important issue — many companies strive for this. The second one is, shareholders have priority. It used to be the employee, in the past; but not anymore. Next one is public relations, which means having good relations with the stakeholders, including the local community.

A: We believe corporate culture is the way of doing things, also an unwritten unit of rules, known within the company. Japanese culture is different from the U.S. one — U.S. is the individual-oriented society, Japan is organization-oriented and it is changing to the U.S. system. Hence the individual will be more important rather than the group efficiency. For making industrial products under the Japanese way of order, harmony is important. Today, product is information-based. We can consider the organization as a whole as an individual. Traditionally, importance was not given to the individual, but today the individual's position is becoming more important. Without talking approval from the boss, people can take decisions.

Q: May be some other features of corporate culture?

A: There are many. One is objective — this can be short term or long term. In the traditional way, long-term objective was very important, but today it is difficult to define long term. Five years may be too long; hence the way of recovering the investment or cost has changed to short-term. Time development — i.e., time needed to develop the product starting from the research stage, has to be shortened. Development of product-manufacturing process has to be shortened. Regarding information and decision-making process resources — in the past a Japanese company wanted to do everything inside — they are outsourcing these now.

Q: They recruit freshmen to establish contact or accumulate clients. Acquiring clients is important; and for this human skills like cooperativeness, optimistic personality are important?

A: Japanese companies do not depend much on the university. On job training and house training are the investments we make for the employees. But this is changing and the skillsets' requirement is changing. Companies procure services when needed. In the traditional way, old employees were retained for cleaning, general work, anything. Today, we cannot have that kind of room as we need to keep the cost low and remain competitive.

Q: Do you think that the role of *Jinjibu* is important?

A: It is changing. The company used to distribute each freshman in April to each division, first. Each will go through job rotations and they acquire general business knowledge. Today, more specialization is needed. They need well-established skills as in the American system. *Jinjibu* is recruiting people, depending on the specific function like legal department for example.

Q: Human features are important — what kind of features?

A: Skills in specified area. In Japan, this is attitude to human relation — for business promotion.

Q: What kind of attitude is welcome?

A: Those who can get well with others.
Good relations and leadership are necessary for manager. Engineering function is required for other different things.

Q: Our hypothesis is, managers determine the organizational culture.

A: Yes, how he will value his subordinates, the expectations from his boss. It makes the culture different.

Q: What expectation they have for subordinates?

A: He can be cooperative. If he wants to finish within time, the subordinate can finish by even working in the weekends. Specialty, capability, and insight.

Q: What kind of training managers have?

A: We cannot generalize — it depends on manufacturing or corporate sides. These functions differ: in legal function training in general, on job training, and then I have foreign study in Pennsylvania, domestic study also. These are seminar programmes.

Q: Who is responsible for on job training?

A: General manager, have supervisors, next to him *Khacho*, who is responsible for implementation. He may be busy, new freshman may work with seniors (*Senpai*). His boss, afterwards, reports to him sometimes and receives suggestions. It is the part of the on job training.

Q: Is there any examination going on in that system?

A: Self-examination — assessment sheets — made by himself and communication with his manager — about what he wants to do.

In the next level, they get examined, then promotion becomes difficult. Today, they have that kind of examination system which was not there in the past.

Q: When this system was established?

A: Long time ago — 20 years ago.

Q: How do you measure performance in the company?

A: Profit and market share are important.

Q: Western approach is different — what is the system used here to measure profit?

A: Japanese company accepts a very low profit rate, but they want to improve. Value added-share between employees, customers, and shareholders' increase of salaries are related to lowering of price to customers. Profit is limited. As a result, total volume of sales goes up. Profit ratio is very low, but sales are big.

Q: Who determines organizational culture?

A: Customers. Government is a major customer — then consumer market — industrial market — company's atmosphere has changed.

Q: In case they want to change, who is responsible for decision-making?

A: Top managers make the guide post — most important is the managing director of the group.

Q: Do they consult with the lower level of managers?

A: Suggestions comes from lower managers — the general condition is maintained by manager.

Q: In our case, we have two models, home and host country models. Do you think organizational culture can be transferred or we need new organizational culture for the host country?

A: We have to make a new organizational culture, but home country will have the influence. It has to be adapted to the local culture. Otherwise it is difficult to manage people.

Q: We covered almost everything. Is there is a particular slogan for the company to determine culture?

A: Yes, customer orientation is the slogan.

Q: Do you have traditional way of *Kaizen*?

A: In manufacturing, we have *Kaizen* in all operations. Most activities are in manufacturing — there efforts are directed for corporate staffs as well.

Q: Thank you so much for your time. The style of this research is to maintain confidentiality. If you allow me I will show you my preliminary analysis.

A: That will be interesting. Thank you.

Comments

Corporate governance system of Japanese MNCs are independent of local rules except in the USA. This is because Japanese MNCs are financially independent and they do not raise finance in the host countries. All these activities increase the degree of control of the head office on the subsidiary, but at the same time may reduce the profitability of the subsidiary if the degree of departure of that host country's local practices are too vast from the Japanese practices. This is the reason for the low profitability of the European and U.S. subsidiaries compared with the subsidiaries in Asia.

Chapter 6

Management System and Organizational Culture

The important question is whether organizational culture of a Japanese multinational is affected by national culture of Japan or whether the culture of a Japanese company can be global. This controversy can be subdivided into two broad categories: (a) sociological analysis and (b) analysis of management systems.

Japanese post-war economic development is related to the uniqueness of Japanese national culture, which has produced a specific organizational culture and as a result high-speed growth. Japan has a unique organizational culture based upon its history and society. Both Japanese companies and Japanese household share a sense of their past, respect for their founders, and an obligation to their future. Individuals are expected to subordinate their personal interests to those of the household or the company to show unwavering loyalty and respect to their seniors.

There is an opinion that Japan due to the influence of its unique national culture has developed a form of capitalism which is different from the "Western capitalism". Japanese culture exhibits consensus, harmony, affective relationships, hierarchy and groupism that are very different from individualism, class conflict, and ruthlessness. These Japanese cultural values are clearly identifiable in the style of the Japanese company, especially in the relationship between management and workers. The fate of workers is closely connected with the company, and socialization into the corporate community reinforces this.

Corporate culture does not reduce or eliminate national differences in multinational corporations. Organizational cultures enhance them in certain cases. For example, multinational companies in the U.S. and Japan may look the same from outside, but the American and Japanese people behave differently within them according to their national culture and as a result organizational culture changes gradually.

In a Japanese organization, control is based on a broad organizational culture. Ouchi (1981) have described this type of organization as Type *J*, which is different from the American style of organization (Type *A*) and the emerging Western global ideal style (Type *Z*). A Type *Z* organization has values, which are shared by the members of the organization, as well as recipes for member's behaviour. Type *A* has explicit formalized control, Type *J* has implicit informal control, and Type *Z* has implicit informal control with explicit formalized measures. In Type *J*, responsibility is collective but in both Type *A* and Type *Z* responsibility is individual. In a Type *A*, subsidiary would have a reasonable flexibility to adapt to the local laws and customs. In both Type *J* and Type *Z* through constant personal interactions with headquarters, members remain in close contact with the rest of the world. A firm of this type transfers its organizational culture to its overseas subsidiary. This is accomplished by an emphasis on use of expatriates, extensive training and socialization, and a high frequency of personal contacts between headquarters and subsidiary. The advantages are low employee turnover and a greater control. The disadvantages are less flexibility for subsidiary management and possible conflict with local culture.

There are two "task contingencies" that middle managers of Japanese firms face: Task uncertainty and task dependence. The former has to do with the gap between the amount of information one has in completing the task and what one already has from one's organizational position. The latter is defined as the gap between information, resources, and other supports that are required to complete the task and those which an organizational position automatically brings to a manager. Task dependence is much more important than task uncertainty. In implementing something new to the organization, he or she needs to obtain information, which is not automatically available to his organizational position.

Thus, a horizontal coordination is needed at the middle management level. Japanese firms use networks to create that coordination at all levels. As each phase is autonomous yet loosely linked, interaction between phases is induced and an abundant sharing of information is promoted in the innovation generation process. The strategic planning style is the dominant management style among Japanese firms. Its key characteristics are networked organizations, which favour organization structures and decision-making processes to encourage networking and information exchange. In Japanese manufacturing companies, the enabling leader provides a framework made up of corporate values and a powerful vision, within which divisions develop their own strategies without detailed direction from the head office. The leader also establishes challenging performance targets, thereby creating pressure for the divisions to find ways of meeting them. This style of leadership exerts a strong influence on the divisions, but enables them to determine their own strategies within the overall corporate framework.

The main emphasis in Japanese strategic planning is on the incremental improvements, covering detailed programmes for new products, cost reduction, quality improvement, productivity, and other operating measures. However, proposals from the divisions are set within the context of the broader corporate vision determined by the top management in the head office.

Corporate head office of Japanese multinational companies discharges the functions of: (a) planning and allocation of resources; (b) control of performance; and (c) central service provision. Japanese firms are equipped with elements facilitating the creation of horizontal information flow. Linkages among divisions, such as shared clients, production technology, etc., are facilitated by the horizontal information flows between the head office and subsidiaries located in different countries. As subsidiaries of Japanese multinational companies seldom participate in the stock market of the host country, it is financially dependent on the head office, and thus head office through both formal and informal networks exerts considerable influences on the subsidiaries to implement its strategic plans.

Japanese manufacturing firms are often characterized by their large overhead staffs. Size in terms of the employee numbers is significantly linked with the information structure in Japanese firms. When the size of a firm is large, it often "duplicates" the functions of the corporate centre at the divisional level, which facilitates the vertical flow of information. While business autonomy is promoted through the divisionalization, the corporate centre in the head office will still be able to "control" or guide the operations at the divisional level, through the personal contact of the corporate managers with their counterparts at the divisions located in different countries. The existence of similar, if not the same, functions at the corporate centre and divisions will make it possible for the staff to move from the centre to the divisions, or *vice versa*. Networking is thus facilitated.

Japanese multinational company is thus a unified company with not so much "localization" of overseas management. This may be in some way unavoidable or sometimes necessary to create in-company communications in a Japanese multinational company. Besides management and technical expertise, personal networking is at the root of the competitive strength of Japanese multinational companies.

Thus, head office of a Japanese corporation has three functions: (a) formulating corporate strategy, (b) building core competencies, and (c) providing expert services. The head office is a research laboratory for management. Successful Japanese companies have about 8% of personnel in their head offices. The interactions between the headquarters and operating units in subsidiaries located in various countries is crucial for strategic leadership. This is particularly important where the product is of high technological nature, which may demand serious marketing efforts and long-term planning.

The discontinuities have emerged in the last decade, since the economic ills of Japan became evident. These include a shift from a growth emphasis to the balancing of multiple goals, the emergence of new forms of competitive strategy in the form of: alliances and cooperation, changing conceptions of careers, relaxation of the centralization of authority, a shift from lifetime employment to employability, larger differentiation of wages and promotion opportunities in the status ladder system, and the increased scope for initiative and consensus. In view of these, it is a serious question whether the head office of a Japanese multinational company can still maintain the effective control over their subsidiaries and maintain the communication networks.

In particular, the level and mode of central control of overseas units, especially their reliance on expatriate managers, could change as firms become more willing to use foreign subsidiaries as sources of innovation and learning rather than as delivery pipelines for domestically designed and developed products.

Toyota's Management of "Head Office and Subsidiary Relationship"

Toyota is considered here as the typical example of a large Japanese multinational company. Toyota is the creator of its famous Toyota management system, which serves as the model for every Japanese company large or small. Toyota has tried to transplant its organizational culture to its subsidiaries abroad and as a result the relationship between the head office and subsidiary is characterized by this transplantation efforts. We have analyzed the Toyota plants in UK, Australia, India, Thailand and found out they have almost identical personnel management system as in Japanese plants of Toyota.

Thus, in Toyota, the aim is to have complete transplantations of the organizational culture from the head office to the subsidiary although because of circumstances it may not be achievable always. Due to the fact that Toyota along with other major Japanese multinational companies are independent of the financial sector of the host countries but depend solely on the home financial sector, the influence of the head office on the subsidiary is supreme.

Although there are high risks of failure to take into account the local environment, the success can yield a substantial competitive advantage in terms of both productivity and quality of the final products. Even in the hybrid version where the subsidiary can have substantial freedom, the basic elements of the Japanese management system are implemented in all

Toyota plants. Thus, Toyota strives to have its mirror images in the subsidiaries by having Japanese associates shadowing the local executives at all levels of the subsidiary. That implies the head office has total control over the subsidiary.

Transplants of Organizational Culture to the Overseas Subsidiaries

By now, Japanese automakers Toyota, Nissan, and Honda are well established in Britain. Through the suppliers they have managed to develop a kind of Keiretsu (already in Britain) through which they transmit their organizational cultures to their suppliers, British, European and Japanese.

Toyota Motor Corporation's purchasing philosophy is enshrined in the 1939 Purchasing Rules, which state:

> "Once nominated as Toyota suppliers, they should be treated as part of Toyota (as branch plants); Toyota shall carry out business with these suppliers without switching to others, and shall make every effort to raise the performance of these suppliers".

Suppliers benefit from relationships that are variously characterized as relational, obligatory, trust-based, and voice-based. Within Toyota, factory "Jishuken" ("kojo jishuken") — an autonomous study group — takes place as a culmination of education and training for Toyota's middle managers and first-line supervisors. "Jishuken" is a closely knit gathering of middle-level production technologists from a stable group of companies, who jointly develop better capabilities for applying Toyota Production System (TPS) through mutual criticism and concrete application.

The purchasing department also relied on bilateral and multilateral modes of supplier development. In the multilateral mode, the department has been in charge of the supplier association, "Kyohokai", which, despite its ever-expanding membership, remains a forum for imparting and sharing information in the supplier community. They hold regular seminars, study group meetings, training courses, exhibitions, and presentations of members' achievements in various matters including cost, quality, delivery, and development.

Toyota Quality Circle (TQC) helped diffuse TPS within each supplier company, contributing to the self-sustainability of capability-enhancement activity. By contrast, the establishment of Nissan's Engineering Support Department and Honda's Purchasing Technical Centre led to the incorporation of supplier assistance in various areas (including quality, logistics, product development, etc.) within the purchasing function. The result is not only diffusion of technology and finance, but also close networks of organizations with similar organizational culture to reduce their transaction costs. That gives distinct competitive advantages to the Japanese automakers in Britain over their American or German counterparts. Collectivism as represented by the organizational culture of Japanese firms can be a very important competitive advantage for a large Japanese multinational company and its networks of supplier firms and thus, it may be responsible for a superior corporate performance. Thus, in the context of a Japanese firm, the organizational culture has certain economic dimensions or resources, which should not be ignored.

The three major Japanese manufacturing and assembly transplants in Great Britain — Nissan, Honda, and Toyota — enjoy the combined services of a large number of Japanese suppliers. At Nissan (UK), the use of traditional Japanese open spaces instead of individual offices so characteristic of North American and European corporations, greatly enhances the exchange of information so essential in high learning and adaptive organizations. All managers are compensated under the same pay systems, resulting in fewer problems and more harmony within the plant. Supervisors at Nissan (UK) are leaders of the team and professionals and are given unusual power and responsibility. They are at the same level as the engineers and controllers. However, they are represented by the same union as the workers, further blurring the line between management and labour. At Nissan (UK), overcoming the infamous British shop steward adversarial culture ("them and us") on the shop floor was particularly critical for the collectivistic Japanese ("just us") lean philosophy and system to succeed.

The organizational capabilities that are being replicated at suppliers consist of a hierarchy of practiced routines that are coherent. One important capability in supplier development is continuous improvement (or *Kaizen*). Continuous improvement is inherently firm-specific in its application and results, and therefore is part of the intangible assets for which no ready market exists. The distinctive and difficult-to-replicate character of such assets is central to the sustenance of a firm's competitive advantage. Suppliers benefit from relationships that are variously characterized as based on relation, obligation, trust, and voice. Long-term trading induces investment in relation-specific skills, a joint problem-solving approach, and a clear rule for sharing gains between the automaker and the supplier. The purpose of the Japanese management system is to create commitment for the organization, and organizational culture plays a very important role.

Management System in India in its Cultural Context

Japanese companies operating in India follow the Japanese system of management. However, as they operate within the influence of the Indian corporate sector, it is essential to understand the difference between the Japanese system of corporate management and the Indian system. Because the senior managerial staffs in the Indian operations of the Japanese multinational companies are drawn from the Indian corporate sector and as a result they may carry with them the Indian system of corporate management.

The management system of the Indian private sector, comprised of more than 86% of the economy reflects the extended family system of India which is hierarchical and less egalitarian than its Western counterparts, but there is an important difference in the Indian private sector. Because of the traditional espoused idea of the government for socialism, although now discarded since 1992, trade unions are very powerful unlike that in either Japan or Thailand. Industrial relations acts are geared to protect the workers, not to enhance the interest of the corporate managers. Despite of that, certain common characteristics of the Indian culture, which form the behavioural pattern of the Indian employees, are observed by a number of researchers. These characteristics are: respect for and obedience to authority, public expression of emotions and feelings, group morality and community orientation, dependence on others, caste orientations, competitiveness, selfishness, and lack of concern for others. Indian people are fatalistic and have low expectations from their organizations, they do not have great commitment to their organizations, and they are not work collectively but for their own individual achievement. Because of very high degree of power distance, employees have few opportunities to participate in any decision-making process. That has intensified the conflict between the management and other employees as there is no trust between them.

The level of communications and consultations regarding the affairs of the organization is absent even in the middle or senior management levels, as a result of family-oriented management system, where all decisions are taken by the family that controls the organization.

Indian management system is highly formal, with Indian managers use direct supervision and personal contacts with shop-floor employees as well as their immediate subordinates. Control over managers and other staff was generally exercised through target setting and progress monitoring; over manual workers through time-keeping and productivity measurement. There is a strong preference for personalized relationship. Excessive dependency is the dominant orientation of the Indian executives. Weak work values and strong status orientations are pervasive. Loyalty is often prioritized over efficiency and intrinsic work vales suffer in such a personalized work culture.

According to Hofstede (in his website www.geert-hofstede.com), India has a very high power distance of dimension 77 compared with the world average of 56.5. That indicated high inequality of power and wealth within the society. This is accepted by the fatalist population as a cultural norm. India's long-term orientation dimension of 61, with the world average of 48, indicates its managerial culture is perseverant and parsimonious. India has masculinity dimension of 56, much above the world average of 51. It indicates that there are high differences between the values of men and women. India has a low ranking in uncertainty avoidance at 40, compared with the world average of 65. The culture is this open to unstructured ideas and situations. The population have fewer rules and regulations to attempt control of unknown and unexpected events.

This system of management in the Indian private sector organization is in sharp contrast with the Japanese system of management and in the management system of the Japanese organizations in India.

Management System in Thailand

Prior to the 1990s, Thailand existed for centuries with little cultural change and was never colonized by another Asian or Western power just like Japan but unlike India which was colonized since 12th century. Thus, the psychology and mental orientations of the Thais are very different from that of the Indians but close to that of the Japanese. We provide a list of espoused values of Thai employers and employees, high or low. These are:

(a) A tradition of spiritualism as based on Buddhism; to give more than one takes; to resist material attachments;
(b) A desire to have trust in business relationship, though traditional, social business networks, built over time;
(c) Need to take care of employees, avoid lay-offs, and protect investors from loss;
(d) Desire to keep the unemployment rate down by preserving low-skilled jobs in labour-intensive export industries;
(e) Desire for face-to-face business contacts, based on trust and confidentiality;
(f) Follow the King's advice to be a more self-sufficient country, to produce what one needs, become less dependent on imports.

Thailand tries to maintain its cultural roots which is collectivist, avoids uncertainty, have power distance, and long-term orientation. According to Hofstede (in his website www.geert-hofstede.com), Thailand has lower score on power distance than other Asian countries, but it is still very high. Thus, it, just like other Asian countries, has high level of inequality of power and wealth within the society and among the employees. It has very low score in individualism, much less than that in Japan. It also has low score in masculinity. Thus, Thais are not competitive or assertive. It has a high score on uncertainty avoidance. Its score of long-term orientation is less than that in other Asian countries or Japan. It has low level of tolerance for uncertainty. As a result, the society is highly regulated and does not accept rapid changes and is very risk averse. The society is collectivist with close long-term commitment to the members of the inner circle. Loyalty is paramount and overrides most other societal rules and regulations. The society fosters strong relationship where everyone takes responsibility for fellow members of their group. The society is less assertive and competitive.

Thais are trained to be humble and *Kreng Jai* (considerations for other's feelings). It is derived from their main religion Buddhism which promotes coexistence, tolerance, and individual initiatives. Although emerging values of materialism are increasingly seen as a sign of success by the new generation, this represents conflict between the old and the new values. The concept of *Kreng Jai* means an individual seeks to avoid potentially traumatic or discomforting situations even when his or her own interests may be compromised.

Most of the business relations in Thailand are based on the concept of *Bun Khun* which implies if someone helps someone, the recipient person will have an obligation to do the same to the provider. Employees or business partners are expected to be treated fairly. Thais, thus, depend upon this concept and expect that a good relationship would emerge anyway in the long term. Thai culture puts emphasis on social and interpersonal harmony which is applicable to the industrial management as well. Thailand scores low on masculinity scale. Employer avoids layoffs or sacking as there is no social security. This is rooted on the value of having empathy for others, which the employees are expected to demonstrate as well in return. This is related to the Thai concept of *Ruam Hau Tai*, which means sharing gains and losses from the beginning to the end. Thus, Thais avoid confrontations at all costs and the management style is paternalistic, which desires for social harmony with empathic relationship between the superiors and the subordinates to create a paternalistic dependency. Thus, subordinates respect authority, where the superiors are expected to take care of the subordinates.

Thais also avoid uncertainty and ambiguity. Most industrial relationships are based on long-term trust and confidentiality. However, Thai business practices and management system differ considerably from those in the Chinese-owned companies in Thailand, which are there for centuries and Chinese are also a part of the Thai society. Thai managers of Chinese origin have different values which are highly materialistic, assertive, and with very high degree of power distances.

Management system of the Japanese subsidiaries follow the Japanese system, not Thai or Chinese–Thai systems. Thus, there are considerable differences between Thai organizations and subsidiaries from Japan regarding not only the management system but also their business practices, as the Japanese companies are well-established in Thailand with the established Keiretsu system which avoid dealing directly with the Thai or Chinese–Thai companies in many ways.

Corporate Management of Japanese Multinational Companies Abroad

The organizational culture of Toyota, Honda, and Mitsubishi would form a company culture throughout their worldwide organizations disregarding national boundaries. These companies have a strong organizational culture, which is rooted in its values, beliefs, and assumptions. To the employees, the company is a living entity. The continuous growth of the company is needed for the preservation of these values. Continuous progress and respect that can be gained when associated with a company with continuous growth is the end objective of the employees. A deep religious value to perpetuate growth is also the objective of the corporate growth. Employees think and operate with their outlook for the long-term prospect of the organization and harmony with the workplace and broad social environment. These feelings lead them to develop a family feeling within the workplace and responsibility towards the fellow employees and the community at large. They believe they have a responsibility towards the organization and the local and global societies, as these companies are now a global organization. Irrespective of the location, these companies are striving to inject these values to their employees across the globe, creating an organization citizenship which would carry the essential values of these companies as global organizations. The fear of loss of face due to non-achievements of its objectives to the employees, to Japan and to the global community are the motives for the efforts of these companies to mould every employee irrespective of their nationality. The then president of Toyota in 1995, Shoichiro Okuda said that his task is "to encourage a change in nationality through globalization — to transform Toyota Motor Corporation into Toyota, a company with a world nationality" (Okuda, 1995). That is also true for Honda and Mitsubishi.

Chapter 7

Quantitative Method to Analyze Corporate Governance

Every corporate governance creates a specific corporate culture and a management system. A number of efforts were undertaken by various researchers to measure the nature of organizational culture and corporate management. However, there is a serious problem of objectivity that exists in area of organizational culture research as in any social sciences' area because of the inherent defects of the sampling methods and statistical inferences. Thus, measurement in social science is only an attempt to obtain some reflections of the truth. However, despite these defects, significant achievements have been made in recent years to design novel methods and models incorporating organizational cultures and their impacts on the company behaviour. Scholars have proposed a large variety of dimensions and attributes of organizational culture. The reason so many dimensions have been proposed is that organizational culture is extremely broad in scope. It implies a complex, interrelated, ambiguous set of factors. No one framework or measurement tool described so far seems to be comprehensive, nor one particular framework or measurement tool can be argued to be right while others are wrong. It is believed that the most appropriate framework and instrument to measure organizational culture should be based on empirical evidence and should be able to integrate most of the dimensions proposed already in the literature.

O'Reilly *et al.* (1991) have created an instrument called *Organizational Culture Profile* (OCP) to measure organizational culture and its characteristics. The way to evaluate culture, according to them, is to focus on the central values that may be important to a worker's self-concept or identity as well as relevant to the organization's central value system. The instrument contains a set of value statements that can be used to idiographically assess both the extent to which certain values characterize a target organization and an individual's preference for that particular configuration of values.

O'Reilly *et al.* (1991) have recommended seven dimensions that could be used to compare across organizations. Some dimensions of organizational culture are as follows:

- Innovation and risk taking — willing to experiment, take risks, encourage innovation;
- Attention to detail — paying attention to being precise vs saying its "good enough for chopped salad";
- Outcome orientation — oriented to results vs oriented to process;
- People orientation — degree of value and respect for people. Are people considered as unique talents, or is an engineer an engineer;
- Individual vs team orientation — are individuals most highly noted, or are collective efforts;
- Aggressiveness — taking action, dealing with conflict;
- Stability — openness to change.

One of the main purposes of these authors was to examine whether a person fits with the organizational culture of his place of employment by comparing it with the ideal organizational culture as imagined by that person. In this research, we have adopted this methodology.

Following the literature, we have identified the following variables for corporate governance:

(1) Community feelings;
(2) Innovations;
(3) *Hou-Ren-Sou*;
(4) Stability;
(5) Employee welfare;
(6) Contributions to organization.

We have identified the following variables for operations management:

(1) Awareness of return to investment;
(2) *Kaizen*;
(3) Total quality management;
(4) Customer satisfaction;
(5) Facilitations;
(6) Goal orientations;
(7) Preciseness;
(8) Emphasis on daily performance.

We have used a number of questionnaires to conduct the surveys among the managers of Toyota, Honda, and Mitsubishi in Japan, Thailand, UK, India, and Australia. After eliminating forms which are incomplete or wrongly filled up, 1,300 answers are selected, 650 from Japan and 650 from Thailand and India each as representative samples for the employees of Toyota, Honda, and Mitsubishi in Japan, Thailand, and India. The sample obtained in this study consists of 650 employees in Japan and 650 employees in Thailand and India each. Responses sought according to a 7-point Likert scale.

We provide below the questionnaire used.

Questionnaire

"Macro Values" Variable

		YES	NO	UNSURE
1.	Religious principles determine macro values of national culture.			
2.	Moral principles determine macro values of national culture.			
3.	Habits determine macro values of national culture.			
4.	Combination of religious, moral and habitual principles determine national culture.			
5.	Moral values are affected by religious values.			

6.	Habitual values are affected by moral values.			
7.	Habitual values are affected by religious values.			
8.	Macro values are related to meso values of organizational culture.			
9.	Macro values influence organizational culture.			
10.	Macro values influences HR practices.			
11.	Macro values influence leader culture.			

"National Culture" Variable

		YES	NO	UNSURE
1.	It is very important for me to have a sense of belonging.			
2.	It is very important for me to have an exciting life.			
3.	It is very important for me to have fun and enjoyment in life.			
4.	It is very important for me to have warm relationships.			
5.	It is very important for me to be self-fulfilled in life.			
6.	It is very important for me to be well-respected.			
7.	It is very important for me to have a sense of life accomplishment.			
8.	It is very important for me to have security.			
9.	It is very important for me to gain self-respect.			
10.	I think that national culture influences organizational culture of my company.			
11.	All top managers in my company are good examples of representatives of my national culture.			
12.	National culture has strong influence on HR practices in my company.			

"Meso Values" Variable

		YES	NO	UNSURE
1.	Meso values in Japanese companies combine *Kaizen*, *Hou-Ren-Sou*, Senpai/Kohai, and conformity approaches.			
2.	Meso values are formed by national culture.			
3.	Meso values influence HR practices in my company.			
4.	Meso values are contributed significantly towards the formation of organizational culture.			
5.	Meso values are formed by national culture.			
6.	Meso values influences HR practices.			
7.	Meso values contribute significantly towards the formation of organizational culture in my company.			
8.	Characteristics of the leadership style are formed by meso values.			
9.	*Kaizen* is the significant part of Meso values in my company.			
10.	I believe that *Hou-Ren-Sou* approach is formed by Senpai/Kohai system.			
11.	Conformity (Nail approach) is influenced by Senpai/Kohai system.			
12.	Senpai/Kohai system is an important part of meso values.			
13.	Conformity (Nail approach) is an essential part of meso values.			

"Organizational Culture" Variable

		YES	NO	UNSURE
1.	We have strong traditions and customs in my company.			
2.	Group norms are essential part of culture in my company.			

3.	I think that espoused values are main traits of the organizational culture of my company.			
4.	Company's mission determines the overall organizational culture in my company.			
5.	Newcomer must learn the rules of the game to become a real member of the collective of people in my company.			
6.	I believe that physical layout determines the climate and thus forms organizational culture in my company.			
7.	I think that emotional climate is a major part of organizational culture in my company.			
8.	Ability to do certain things better than others is the major trait of organizational culture.			
9.	I think that my co-workers and myself help each other to understand and develop new ideas.			
10.	I believe that having similar habits of thinking is the major trait of organizational culture.			
11.	People rather stay in one workplace forever rather than apply elsewhere, because my organization is like a family for me.			
12.	We have a multicultural collective of people working in my organization.			
13.	Our organization mostly consists of people of the same nationality and culture.			

Interrelationship Between Corporate Governance System and Corporate Performance

		YES	NO	UNSURE
1.	I think that only the companies with strong organizational culture have good corporate performance.			
2.	There is a link between strength of the company's culture and its net income growth.			

3.	I think that every employee determines the organizational culture in my company.			
4.	I think that the top managers only determine the organizational culture for my company.			
5.	There is link between strength of the company's culture and return of investment.			
6.	Only insider can become a top manager in my company.			
7.	The organizational culture helped to improve my company's overall performance over the last 20 years.			
8.	The culture of my company values customers.			
9.	The culture of my company values employees.			
10.	I think that my company is focused on the product of my company.			
11.	I believe that there is a link between the risk-taking behaviour of my company and the basic organizational values of my company.			
12.	There is a link between the marketing efficiency of my company and organizational values.			

Operations Management System

		5	4	3	2	1
1.	Emphasis on on job training.					
2.	Emphasis on pre-qualification of recruits.					
3.	Emphasis on personality of recruits.					
4.	Emphasis on employee welfares.					
5.	Emphasis on job itself.					
6.	Emphasis on parochialism in selection process.					
7.	Collective bargaining system in wage determinations.					
8.	Trade union militancy.					

9.	Emphasis on political ideology.					
10.	Performance-based wage system.					
11.	Just-in-time inventory system.					
12.	Total quality management.					
13.	Relationship with suppliers.					
14.	Locations of the suppliers.					
15.	Factory layout.					
16.	Robotics and other information technology in productions.					
17.	Awareness of changes in preferences of the consumers.					
18.	Distribution system.					
19.	Relationship with subsidiaries overseas.					
20.	Transfer pricing system with the subsidiaries overseas.					

Chapter 8

Results of the Surveys

The result of these surveys conducted in Toyota, Honda, and Mitsubishi in Japan, UK, Thailand, and India are summarized into forms which can be analyzed in future publications. Because the data collected so far are of small samples, we have decided to merge data according to the country of origin. As a result, we have good enough data samples from Japan, India, and Thailand, but not enough from UK and very little from Australia. As a result, this research will concentrate only on the samples from Japan, India, and Thailand. We have identified certain key variables to characterize the corporate governance system and operations management; we provide here the initial statistical analysis.

We have identified the following variables for corporate governance:

(1) Community feelings;
(2) Innovations;
(3) *Hou-Ren-Sou*;
(4) Stability;
(5) Employee welfare;
(6) Contributions to organization;
(7) Decisiveness;
(8) Communications and supportiveness.

We have identified the following variables for Operations management:

(1) Awareness of return to investment;
(2) *Kaizen*;
(3) Total quality management;
(4) Customer satisfaction;
(5) Facilitations;
(6) Goal orientations.

The Characteristics of the Sample for Japan

In the Japanese sample, employees have long tenure (see Table 1). That would mean the employees in Japan have longer time to absorb the organizational culture. There are very few foreigners if any at all. The employees are almost all men, there are few females. Most of the Japanese employees have not received training in cultural adaptations or foreign language because most of them would not be posted abroad.

Table 1.   Japanese sample.

Items	Employees in Japan
Number of respondents	650
Gender	Male = 642; Female = 8
Tenure	
Length of service (mean)	17.25 years
Age	
Under 35	27.5%
35–45	64.5%
Above 45	8%
Educational level	
Senior high school	12.0%
University graduate	79.5%
Post graduate	8.5%

(*Continued*)

Table 1. (*Continued*)

Items	Employees in Japan
Nationality	
Japanese	98%
Thai	0%
Other Asian	2%
Formal cultural training	
Posted abroad	4.5%
Received cultural training	15.6%
Received language training	13.6%

The Characteristics of the Sample for Thailand

In Table 2, the samples of Thailand are provided. In Thailand, majority of the employees are younger than those in Japan. Regarding education, Thai employees are more educated than the Japanese, although quality of Thai education may differ. There are very few foreigners, except for the Japanese, in this operation in Thailand. The employees are almost all men; there are few females. Most the employees in Thailand have received cultural adaptation training and Japanese language training as part of their training for the company. They have to go to Japan from time-to-time for further training.

The Characteristics of the Sample for India

In the Japanese sample, employees have long tenure. In the Indian subsidiary, they have no more than 10 years' tenure (see Table 3). That would mean the employees in Japan have longer time to absorb the organizational culture than their counterparts in India. There are no foreigners except for the Japanese. The employees are almost all men, there are few females. A lot of the employees have received training in cultural adaptations or Japanese language and about 500 of them went to Japan for training.

The mean responses are more or less about 5.5 on the average in the Likert's scale of 7. The only exception is that of OCJV5 (Employee Welfare)

Table 2.   Characteristics of the sample for Thailand.

Items	Employees in Thailand
Number of respondents	650
Gender	Male = 638; Female = 12
Tenure	
Length of service (mean)	9.35 years
Age	
Under 35	39.6%
35–45	56.7%
Above 45	3.7%
Educational level	
Senior high school	1.1%
University graduate	91.5%
Post graduate	7.4%
Nationality	
Japanese	0.1%
Thai	98.5%
Other Asian	1.4%
Formal cultural training	
Posted abroad	1.7%
Received cultural training	73.1%
Received language training	42.5%

Table 3.   Indian sample.

Items	Employees in India
Number of respondents	650
Gender	Male = 642; Female = 8
Tenure	
Length of service (mean)	7.25 years
Age	
Under 35	37.5%
35–45	61.5%
Above 45	1%

(Continued)

Table 3. (*Continued*)	
Items	Employees in India
Educational level	
Senior high school	2.0%
University graduate	79.5%
Post graduate	18.5%
Nationality	
Indian	99%
Japanese	less than 1%
Other Asian	0%
Formal cultural training	
Posted abroad	1.5%
Received cultural training	55.6%
Received language training	13.6%

which is little less than others with 4.24. It is possible that due to the economic crisis of Japan, MNCs are reorganizing their work force and that may cause them to be less coherent and supportive towards the welfare of the employees than they used to be before. From the responses, we can say that this research has identified the eight major components of corporate governance, as the responses for these components from the employees are of higher values (close to the maximum of 7) and these are statistically significant with very little standard errors for the means.

Factor Analysis: Japan

Factor analysis is used here to uncover the latent structure or dimensions of a set of variables estimated from the scores obtained from the survey of opinions of the employees in Japan and Thailand. Here, the analysis of the perceived ideas of the employees they experience in Japan is presented (see Table 4). Factor analysis reduces attribute space from a larger number of variables to a smaller number of factors and as such is a "non-dependent" procedure. In other words, it does not assume that a dependent variable is specified. Here, in this research, the purpose

Table 4.   Factor analysis: Corporate governance in Japan.

Factor Loadings	Innovation	Employee Welfare	Communality
Community feeling	0.967	0.117	0.976
Innovations	0.116	0.960	0.951
Hou-Ren-Sou	0.965	0.018	0.948
Stability	0.954	0.151	0.973
Employee welfare	0.101	0.960	0.984
Contributions to organization	0.986	0.150	0.945
Decisiveness	0.977	0.029	0.963
Communications	0.945	0.116	0.952
Eigen value	6.013	1.657	
Percent variance explained	75.264	23.227	

KMO and Bartlett's Test.

Kaiser–Meyer–Olkin Measure of Sampling Adequacy		0.819
Bartlett's Test of Sphericity	Approx. Chi-square	14,444.581
	df	28
	Sig.	0.000

of factor analysis is to reduce a large number of variables to a smaller number of factors for modelling purposes, where the large number of variables precludes modelling all the measures individually. As such, factor analysis in this research is integrated in Structural Equation Modelling (SEM) presented later, helping to confirm the latent variables modelled by SEM.

Here, the Exploratory Factor Analysis (EFA) is carried on to find out which factors are relatively more important to influence corporate governance in Japanese multinational companies. Confirmatory Factor Analysis (CFA) will be used in the SEM framework later to confirm our theory that there is a close relationship between corporate governance and operations management.

Table 5.   Results of factor analysis on corporate governance in Japan.

Most Important Factors	Related To
1. Employee welfare	Innovations
2. Innovation	Community feeling, *Hou-Ren-Sou*, Contributions to organization, decisiveness, communications

EFA seeks to uncover the underlying structure of a relatively large set of variables. The researcher's *"à priori"* assumption is that any indicator may be associated with any factor. This is the most common form of factor analysis. There is no prior theory, and one uses factor loadings intuitively to explore the factor structure of the data.

The communality measures the percent of variance in a given variable explained by all the factors jointly and may be interpreted as the reliability of the indicator. High communalities here indicate that all factors are very good indicators of the variable, operations management.

The Kaiser criterion suggests that, we can retain only factors with eigen values greater than 1. In this case, only two factors satisfy that criteria, innovations and employee welfare. Thus, these two factors are fundamental in Japanese corporate governance (see Table 5).

Operations Management in Japan

From the above statistics, it is clear that the assumptions of normal distributions of the variables can be maintained, as both the skewness and Kurtosis are within valid range. As a result, most of the testing procedures in factor analysis and regression analysis will be valid. High scores of goal orientations (OCOMJV6) and awareness of return to investment (OCOMJV1) show that employees in Japan are enterprising to satisfy the purpose of the organization and operations management styles demonstrate that. They rationalize these psychological factors in terms of *Kaizen* and facilitations, the other two factors receiving high attention. Very high scores imply that the operations management policy is emphasizing these aspects.

Factor Analysis on Operations Management

Factor analysis is used here to uncover the latent structure or dimensions of a set of variables estimated from the scores obtained from the perceived ideas of the employees regarding the operations management policy they experience in Japan. Factor analysis reduces attribute space from a larger number of variables to a smaller number of factors and as such is a "non-dependent" procedure. Here, the EFA is carried on to find out which factors are relatively more important to influence operations management in Japanese multinational companies like Toyota, Honda, and Mitsubishi in Japan.

The communality measures the percent of variance in a given variable explained by all the factors jointly and may be interpreted as the reliability of the indicator. High communalities here indicate that all factors are very good indicators of the variable, operations management.

The eigen value for a given factor measures the variance in all the variables, which is accounted for by that factor. The ratio of eigen values is the ratio of explanatory importance of the factors with respect to the variables. If a factor has a low eigen value, then it is contributing little to the explanation of variances in the variables and may be ignored as redundant with more important factors. Here, three indicators have significant eigen values. Thus, these three indicators, *Kaizen*, facilitations, and total quality management are very important to influence the variable operations management (see Tables 6 and 7).

Table 6.   Factor analysis on operations management in Japan.

Factor Loadings	*Kaizen*	Facilitations	Total Quality Management	Communality
Return to investment	0.011	0.004	0.761	0.673
Kaizen	0.951	0.128	0.111	0.962
Total quality management	0.135	0.978	0.013	0.916
Customer satisfaction	0.008	0.954	0.013	0.913
Facilitations	0.950	0.012	0.011	0.907
Goal orientations	0.104	0.004	0.629	0.464
Eigen value	2.319	1.526	1.214	
Percent variance explained	34.969	22.241	15.877	

KMO and Bartlett's Test.

Kaiser–Meyer–Olkin Measure of Sampling Adequacy.		0.534
Bartlett's Test of Sphericity	Approx. Chi-square	2,012.872
	df	15
	Sig.	0.000

Table 7. Main results of factor analysis in operational management in Japan.

Most Important Factors	Related To
Kaizen	Facilitations
Facilitations	Total quality management
Total quality management	Return to investment
	Goal orientation

SEM for Japan: Relationship Between Corporate Governance and Operations Management

SEM using LISREL is used in this research to evaluate the relationships between two unobserved variables corporate governance and operations management for Toyota, Honda, and Mitsubishi in Japan.

CFA seeks to determine if the number of factors and the loadings of measured (indicator) variables on them conform to what is expected on the basis of the pre-established theory. Indicator variables are selected on the basis of prior theory and factor analysis is used to see if they load as predicted on the expected number of factors. The researcher's *à priori* assumption is that each factor (the number and labels of which may be specified *à priori*) is associated with a specified subset of indicator variables. CFA can mean the analysis of alternative measurement (factor) models using a SEM package such as LISREL.

The Method

SEM serves purposes similar to multiple regression, but in a more powerful way which takes into account the modelling of interactions, multiple latent independents each measured by multiple indicators, and one or more latent dependents also each with multiple indicators. SEM is used as a more powerful alternative to multiple regression, path analysis, factor analysis, time series analysis, and analysis of covariance. That is, these procedures may be seen as special cases of SEM, and SEM is an extension of the General Linear Model (GLM) of which multiple regression is a part.

The SEM process has two steps: validating the measurement model and fitting the structural model. The former is accomplished through CFA, while the latter is accomplished primarily through path analysis with latent variables. The measurement model is that part (possibly all) of a SEM model which deals with the latent variables and their indicators. A pure measurement model is a CFA model, in which there is unmeasured covariance between each possible pair of latent variables, there are straight arrows from the latent variables to their respective indicators, there are straight arrows from the error and disturbance terms to their respective variables, but there are no direct effects (straight arrows) connecting the latent variables.

The structural model is the set of exogenous and endogenous variables in the model, together with the direct effects (straight arrows) connecting them, any correlations among the exogenous variable or indicators, and the disturbance terms for these variables, reflecting the effects of unmeasured variables not in the model.

LISREL provides several methods for examining the efficacy of a model which include a chi-square test, goodness-of-fit indices, the distribution of residuals, and a range of other criteria. The hypothesized model discussed before is implemented with the spirit of confirmatory SEM. All the variables are continuous variables satisfying normality criteria.

The path diagram of the relationship between corporate governance and operations management in Japan is given in Figure 1, which shows a high degree of relationship (0.98).

The details of the SEM for Japan are given in Table 8.

Factor scores regression tells us how closely the values of corporate governance are related to the unobserved variable operations management, and which values are relatively more important, taking into account the total effects of all variables on the unobserved variables. Thus, it is a

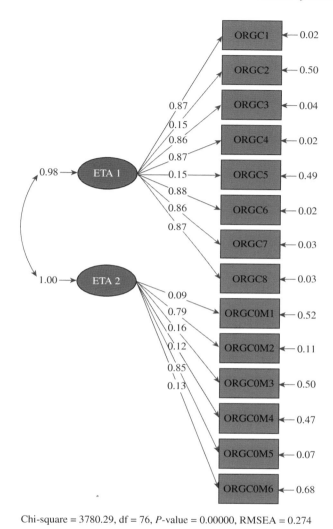

Chi-square = 3780.29, df = 76, *P*-value = 0.00000, RMSEA = 0.274

Figure 1.   Relationship between corporate governance and operations management, Japan.

superior method to examine whether our construct for the unobserved variable are correct or not. Here, we can see that almost all components of corporate governance have high scores to represent the organizational culture. However, for operations management, *Kaizen* and facilitations have high scores to represent the operations management.

Table 8.   Factor scores regressions: Standardized solution (Japan).

	Corporate Governance	Operations Management
Community feelings	0.85	
Innovations	0.15	
Hou-Ren-Sou	0.86	
Stability	0.87	
Employee welfare	0.15	
Contributions to organization	0.88	
Decisiveness	0.86	
Communications	0.87	
Return to investment		0.09
Kaizen		0.79
Total quality management		0.16
Customer satisfaction		0.12
Facilitations		0.85
Goal orientation		0.13

Notes: Chi-square = 5,272.11 ($P = 0.0$); Normed Chi-square = 3,780.29 ($P = 0.0$).
RMSEA = 0.14; Standardized RMR = 0.14; CFI = 0.91; IFI = 0.85.

Table 9.   Correlation matrix.

	Corporate Governance	Operations Management
Corporate governance	1.00	
Operations management	0.98	1.00

Correlation matrix of ETA in LISREL output is the matrix of correlations of the latent dependent and latent independent variables. ETA is a coefficient of nonlinear correlation indicating the degree of relationship. Thus, 0.98 is the correlation between corporate governance and operations management in the sample for Japan (see Table 9). As it is very high, we may conclude there is a very close relationship between corporate governance and operations management in Toyota, Honda, and Mitsubishi companies in Japan.

Analysis of Corporate Governance in the Subsidiaries of Toyota, Honda, and Mitsubishi in Thailand

This research will try to find out how the Japanese multinational companies exert their control on the subsidiaries to transfer the operations management practices of the parent company through the transmission of its home corporate governance culture to the subsidiary, and how that affects the operations management practices in the subsidiary companies.

We have repeated the quantitative method we have applied for Japan on the samples for Thailand as well, which was collected from the Toyota, Honda, and Mitsubishi companies in Thailand. The purpose here is to examine whether we can get the same relationship between corporate governance and operations management as we have seen in Japan. Because the subsidiaries in Thailand are financially dependent upon their parent companies in Japan, the corporate governance system is the same in Thailand as in Japan. Tables 10–15 provide more details.

Similarly, we have performed quantitative analysis on the sample for operations management, and the results from the factor analysis are given in Table 14.

Structural Equation Model for Thailand: Relationship Between Corporate Governance and Operations Management

The purpose of this research is to examine whether a multinational company can transmit its corporate governance culture successfully to its overseas subsidiaries. Examining the opinions expressed by the employees of the Thai subsidiaries of this Japanese organization, it is possible to evaluate the following hypothesis:

> H: There is a strong relationship between corporate governance and operations management in the Thai subsidiaries of Toyota, Honda, and Mitsubishi under our study.

Table 10.   Basic statistics for corporate governance, Thailand.

	N	Mean		Skewness		Kurtosis	
	Statistic	Statistic	Std. Error	Statistic	Std. Error	Statistic	Std. Error
OCTHV1	650	4.9308	3.456E-02	0.067	0.096	-0.019	0.191
OCTHV2	650	4.6846	2.939E-02	-0.271	0.096	-0.152	0.191
OCTHV3	650	4.8338	3.295E-02	0.040	0.096	0.064	0.191
OCTHV4	650	4.8338	3.288E-02	0.022	0.096	0.033	0.191
OCTHV5	650	4.6862	2.929E-02	-0.264	0.096	-0.152	0.191
OCTHV6	650	5.1462	3.370E-02	-0.154	0.096	-0.479	0.191
OCTHV7	650	5.1508	3.363E-02	-0.177	0.096	-0.489	0.191
OCTHV8	650	5.1446	3.353E-02	-0.163	0.096	-0.469	0.191
Valid N (listwise)	650						

Descriptive Statistics

Table 11.   Factor analysis, corporate governance, Thailand.

Factor Loadings	Contribution To Organization	Decisiveness	Communications	Communality
Community feeling	0.001	0.140	0.115	0.003
Innovations	0.002	0.995	0.002	0.992
Hou-Ren-Sou	0.003	0.001	0.995	0.993
Stability	0.004	0.002	0.996	0.994
Employee welfare	0.001	0.996	0.002	0.992
Contributions to organization	0.997	0.002	0.002	0.996
Decisiveness	0.998	0.002	0.001	0.996
Communications	0.997	0.003	0.002	0.995
Eigen value	3.025	2.013	1.954	
Percent variance explained	37.808	25.157	24.423	

Table 12.   Analysis of factor analysis, corporate governance, Thailand.

Most Important Factors	Related To
Contributions to organization	Decisiveness, communications
Decisiveness	Employee welfare, innovations
Communications	Stability, *Hou-Ren-Sou*

The results of the SEM give the following test statistics, from which it is possible to understand the nature of the solution in order to evaluate the above hypothesis.

Factor scores regression tells us how closely the values of organizational culture are related to the unobserved variable organizational culture and which values are relatively more important, taking into account the total effects of all variables on the unobserved variables (see Table 16). Thus, it is a superior method to examine whether our construct for the unobserved variable is correct or not. Here, we can see that *Hou-Ren-Sou* and stability have higher scores to represent the corporate governance.

Table 13.   Basic statistics for operations management, Thailand.

	N	Mean		Skewness		Kurtosis	
	Statistic	Statistic	Std. Error	Statistic	Std. Error	Statistic	Std. Error
OCOMTHV1	650	4.8231	3.210E-02	-0.087	0.096	-0.091	0.191
OCOMTHV2	650	5.3862	2.994E-02	0.388	0.096	-0.164	0.191
OCOMTHV3	650	4.6200	2.852E-02	-0.362	0.096	-0.070	0.191
OCOMTHV4	650	5.9954	3.013E-02	-0.197	0.096	-0.773	0.191
OCOMTHV5	650	4.6354	2.916E-02	-0.268	0.096	0.081	0.191
OCOMTHV6	650	6.0677	3.439E-02	-0.545	0.096	-0.613	0.191
Valid N (listwise)	650						

Descriptive Statistics

Table 14.   Factor analysis, operations management, Thailand.

Factor Loadings	Total Quality Management	Facilitations	Kaizen	Communality
Return to investment	0.003	0.008	0.764	0.592
Kaizen	0.001	0.756	0.154	0.595
Total quality management	0.991	0.002	0.002	0.983
Customer satisfaction	0.004	0.720	0.170	0.549
Facilitations	0.990	0.001	0.003	0.982
Goal orientation	0.007	0.005	0.649	0.430
Eigen value	1.981	1.116	1.035	
Percent variance explained	33.022	18.594	17.242	

Table 15.   Analysis of factor analysis, Thailand.

Most Important Factors	Related To
Total quality management	Facilitations
Facilitations	Customer satisfaction, Kaizen
Kaizen	Return to investment

Table 16.   Factor scores regressions: Standardized solution, Thailand.

	Corporate Governance	Operations Management
Community feelings	0.05	
Innovations	0.01	
Hou-Ren-Sou	0.84	
Stability	0.82	
Employee welfare	0.01	
Contributions to organization	0.05	

(*Continued*)

Table 16.   (*Continued*)

	Corporate Governance	Operations Management
Decisiveness	0.05	
Communications	0.05	
Return to investment		0.86
Kaizen		0.20
Total quality management		0.01
Customer satisfaction		0.03
Facilitations		0.13
Goal Orientation		0.15

Notes: Chi-square = 5,304.34 (*P* = 0.0); Normed Chi-square = 3,189.60 (*P* = 0.0).
RMSEA= 0.14; Standardized RMR= 0.12; CFI = 0.90; IFI = 0.90.

Return to investment and *Kaizen* have higher scores to represent the operations management in Thailand. Thus, these factors are most important to represent corporate governance and operations management in Thailand and these, in effect, represent the effects of particular national and societal culture of Thailand (Figure 2).

Correlation matrix of ETA in LISREL output is the matrix of correlations of the latent dependent operations management (ORGCOM) and latent independent variable corporate governance (ORGC). ETA is a coefficient of nonlinear correlation indicating the degree of relationship. Thus, 0.94 is the correlation between corporate governance and operations management in the sample for Thailand (Table 17). As it is very high, we may conclude there is a very close relationship between corporate governance and operations management in Thailand in Toyota, Honda, and Mitsubishi.

The latent variables in SEM are similar to factors in factor analysis, and the indicator variables likewise have loadings on their respective latent variables. ORGC3 (*Hou-Ren-Sou*) and ORGC4 (Stability) have great effects on corporate governance of Thailand. Similarly, for the latent variable operations management, ORGCOM1 (awareness of return to investment emotional attachment) has a significant effect.

Thus, considering the results of the measurement models and the path diagrams for both Japanese operations and Thai operations, it is justified

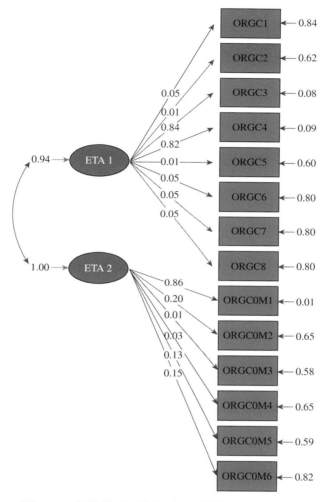

Chi-square = 3189.60, df = 76, *P*-value = 0.00000, RMSEA = 0.251

Figure 2. Relationship between corporate governance and operations management, Thailand.

Table 17. Correlation matrix.

	Corporate Governance	Operations Management
Corporate governance	1.00	
Operations management	0.94	1.00

to accept the hypotheses. Thus, in both Japan and in the Thai subsidiaries, the relationship between corporate governance and operations management is very strong.

Analysis of the Subsidiaries in India

Recent Japanese investments in India have a large proportion of investment in high value-added products and processes, due to the improved productivity and development of supporting industries in Japan itself. A number of Japanese companies have raised the local content of their products while reducing their dependency on the supply of parts and components from Japan. A virtuous cycle between the inflows of Japanese foreign direct investments and industrial development in India may be firmly in place.

The Japanese MNCs in India have adopted the "Growing Together" philosophy of their parent companies to create long-term business growth. In this way, it aims to further contribute to progress in the Indian automotive industry, realize greater employment opportunities for local citizens, improve the quality of life of the team members, and promote robust economic activity in India. Japanese MNCs firmly believe that employees are the main source of strength for the organization. The human resources management seeks to create a corporate culture where values, such as "Continuous Improvement" and "Respect for People", are fully reflected in all actual corporate and individual activities. The companies take maximum care to ensure stability of employment and strive to improve working conditions.

To develop human resources and improve the technical skills of its employees, their young team members are regularly sent to Japan, Indonesia, and Taiwan for training programs. They also believe in continuously improving its products and practices. Every team member is encouraged to give suggestions to improve the product, efficiency of process, or working conditions. They are also appropriately rewarded for the same.

There are close similarities between the corporate management system and operations management system of the Japanese MNCs in Japan and its subsidiaries in India. It signifies that although these

(Toyota and Honda) are new companies in India about 20 years old, organizational culture is very similar and the mentality of the managers are not very different from their Japanese counterparts, despite the vast differences of their culture. Thus, they have managed to surpass the national differences to implement their operations management system in Indian plants as they did across the globe. As these companies depend on their parent companies in Japan for finance, corporate governance systems in India for these companies are identical with their counterparts in Japan (see Tables 18 and 19).

For India, this research has followed exactly the same definitions of values and the corresponding items as given in the questionnaires for

Table 18.   Factor analysis, corporate governance, India.

Factor Loadings	Community Feeling	Innovations	*Hou-Ren-Sou*	Communality
Community feelings	0.000	0.998	0.002	0.997
Innovations	0.000	0.999	0.002	0.999
Hou-Ren-Sou	0.000	0.998	0.002	0.997
Stability	0.008	0.003	0.581	0.346
Employee welfare	0.008	0.000	0.815	0.672
Contributions to organization	0.997	0.000	0.001	0.994
Decisiveness	0.997	0.000	0.001	0.995
Communications	0.997	0.000	0.001	0.994
Eigen value	3.027	2.965	1.000	
Percent variance explained	37.841	37.068	12.502	

Table 19.   Analysis of factor analysis, corporate governance, India.

Most Important Factors	Related To
Community feeling	Communications, decisiveness, Contribution to organization
Innovations	Community feeling, *Hou-Ren-Sou*
Hou-Ren-Sou	Employee welfare, decisiveness

Thailand and Japan. 200 questionnaires were distributed to the employees in India. The sample obtained in this study consisted of 150 employees of Toyota and Honda in India. Responses were sought according to a 7-point Likert scale. Sets of the questionnaire kit were given to the employees in India of this Japanese MNC randomly. Respondents were randomly selected to have a maximum representation from all areas of operations.

Thus, we can have the following observation for organizational culture in the Japanese subsidiary in India:

In the Japanese subsidiaries in India, operational characteristics (Community feelings, innovations, and Hou-Ren-Sou) are very important parts of the corporate governance.

Operational characteristics of the organizational culture in the Japanese subsidiary in India just like in Thailand are related closely to the human resources management policy and strategic management policy.

Human resources practices have their reflections on factors like community feelings, *Hou-Ren-Sou*, employee welfare. Strategic management practices have their reflections on innovation and decisiveness. These factors are in the Indian subsidiary, as these are in the Thai subsidiary, and are related to the operational factors. Thus, operational factors in this Indian subsidiary are reflections of the human resources practice and strategic management policy of the parent unit who decides the characteristics of these two important functions.

Factor Analysis

Factor analysis is used here to uncover the latent structure or dimensions of a set of variables estimated from the scores obtained from the perceived ideas of the Indian employees regarding the corporate governance they experience in the subsidiary operations of these Japanese multinational companies, Toyota and Honda (see Table 20). Here, the EFA is carried on to find out which factors are relatively more

Table 20. Factor analysis, operations management, India.

Factor Loadings	Return to Investment	Customers Satisfaction	Total Quality Management	Communality
Return to investment	0.999	0.000	0.002	1.000
Kaizen	0.004	0.007	0.729	0.539
Total quality management	0.001	0.993	0.001	0.987
Customer satisfaction	0.999	0.000	0.002	1.000
Facilitations	0.000	0.993	0.001	0.987
Goal orientation	0.001	0.009	0.695	0.492
Eigen value	2.023	1.970	1.010	
Percent variance explained	33.722	32.833	16.841	

Table 21. Analysis of the factor analysis, operations management, India.

Most Important Factors	Related To
Return to investment	Customer satisfaction
Customer satisfaction	Total quality management, facilitations
Total quality management	*Kaizen*, goal orientation

important to influence operations management in Japanese multinational companies in India.

High communalities (more than 0.5 or about 0.5) here indicate that almost all factors are very good indicators of the variable, operations management (see Table 21).

Structural Equation Model for India: Relationship Between Corporate Governance and Operations Management

The purpose of this research is to examine whether a multinational company can transmit its organizational culture successfully to its overseas

Table 22.   Factor scores regressions: Standardized solution, India.

	Corporate Governance	Operations Management
Community feelings	0.52	
Innovations	0.52	
Hou-Ren-Sou	0.52	
Stability	0.10	
Employee welfare	0.10	
Contributions to organization	0.13	
Decisiveness	0.12	
Communications	0.09	
Return to investment		0.49
Kaizen		0.23
Total quality management		0.49
Customers satisfaction		0.58
Facilitations		0.25
Goal orientation		0.20

Notes: Chi-square = 1,188.80 (P = 0.0); Normed Chi-square = 1,133.41 (P = 0.0).
RMSEA = 0.15; Standardized RMR = 0.12; CFI = 0.93; IFI = 0.93.

subsidiaries (see Table 22). Examining the opinion expressed by the employees of that Indian subsidiary of this Japanese organization, it is possible to evaluate the following hypothesis:

H: *There is a strong relationship between organizational culture and organizational commitment in the Indian subsidiary of the Japanese organization under our study.*

The results of the SEM give the following test statistics, from which it is possible to understand the nature of the solution in order to evaluate the above hypothesis.

Correlation matrix in LISREL output is the matrix of correlations of the latent dependent and latent independent variables. It gives a coefficient of nonlinear correlation indicating the degree of relationship.

Table 23. Correlation matrix of SEM, India.

	Corporate Governance	Operations Management
Corporate governance	1.00	
Operations management	0.92	1.00

Thus, 0.92 is the correlation between corporate governance and operations management in the sample for India, which is a little lower than that in Thailand and Japan (see Table 23). Close relationship between corporate governance and operations management in India, as perceived by the employees of the Japanese MNCs, is thus established according to the structural equation model for India (Figure 3).

The latent variables in SEM are similar to factors in factor analysis and the indicator variables likewise have loadings on their respective latent variables. ORGC1 (Community feelings), ORGC2 (Innovations), and ORGC3 (*Hou-Ren-Sou*) have great effects on corporate governance of India. Similarly, for the latent variable operations management, ORGCOM1 (awareness of return to investment) and ORGCOM4 (customers satisfaction) have a significant effect.

Factor scores regression tells us how closely the values of corporate governance are related to the unobserved variable corporate governance and which values are relatively more important, taking into account the total effects of all variables on the unobserved variables. Thus, it is a superior method to examine whether our construct for the unobserved variable are correct or not. Here, we can see that community feelings, innovations, and *Hou-Ren-Sou* have higher scores to represent the corporate governance. Awareness of return to investment and customer satisfaction have higher scores to represent the operations management. Thus, these factors are most important to represent corporate governance and operations management in India and these, in effect, represent the effects of particular national and societal culture of India.

Thus, considering the results of the measurement models and the path diagrams for SEM for Indian operations, it is justified to accept the hypotheses that, in the Indian subsidiaries, the relationship between corporate governance and operations management is very strong.

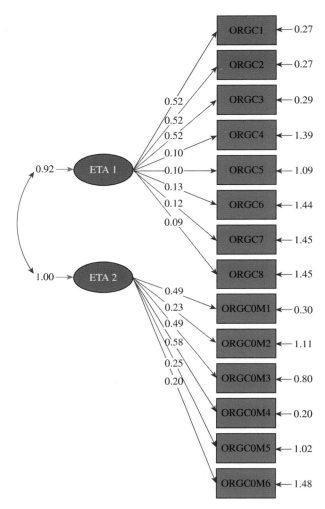

Chi-square = 1133.41, df = 76, *P*-value = 0.00000, RMSEA = 0.146

Figure 3.   Relationship between corporate governance and operations management, India.

Practical implications are that, for building and harnessing local advantages, multinational companies have to bridge cultural, knowledge, and skill gaps between the local and expatriate employees. The actions of these companies have to demonstrate long-term commitment to host countries. CEOs of multinational companies, particularly Asian subsidiaries, can from these studies learn how to build and harness local advantages for global competitiveness.

Considering these results and considering the closeness of the corporate governance of Japan and the Indian subsidiary, it is essential to accept the final observation that the Japanese companies under this study have successfully transmitted their original Japanese corporate governance to their Indian subsidiary overcoming the constraints of existing Indian corporate Governance in the private and the public sectors, and has created the same quality of operations management in its overseas subsidiary as it is in its home operation.

Comments

The literature on organizational culture revealed that the expatriate managers in the MNCs are anticipated to learn and identify the work values and cultural behaviours of the employees within the organization and try to adapt to that culture across the countries. National cultures of the host nations are not a barrier for foreign subsidiaries to operate abroad but in certain cases it may be beneficial due to the common elements. In this case, there are some similarities in the religious background as Buddhism originated from Hinduism and both religions have similar values.

Employee involvement can supplement strong corporate cultures to develop innovative organizations. The system of management evolved from the organizational culture of the Japanese multinational company in India has promoted, as the results demonstrate, a corporate governance culture that is highly related to the motivation of the employees.

Opportunism in organization may be understood in terms of how the self-interests of employers and employees are related to each other. When the employers and employees believe that their goals are competitively but not cooperatively related, they are tempted to pursue their self-interests opportunistically, which is very common in any Indian organizations. However, for this Japanese subsidiary, cognitive understandings and values of a shared vision may have helped employers and employees to believe that their values are cooperatively related. Shared vision can help employees and employers to develop cooperative values that lead to low levels of opportunism and higher level of commitment.

Values are a central part of the culture of the organization. Values emphasize the aspirations of the organization for what it considers ideal. This research on Indian subsidiary has demonstrated the interdependence of values of the employees and the parent organization as created by the organizational culture. The organizational culture adapted from the parent company inspires the employees to work persistently and creatively. Values that convey a deep concern for employees as individuals help to reinforce the purpose of the organization and strengthen the trust and relationships among diverse people. With the affirmation of people values, employees are expected to exchange ideas and abilities with each other. Indian employees, as they are reasonably collectivist with a strong emphasis on subordination and maintaining relationships, are expected to be particularly motivated to demonstrate their loyalty to an employer who cares. Given this sensitivity, they seek harmony.

With a specific and common task, people from different departments appreciate that by working together they can contribute importantly to the organization. Cross-functional teams are given a specific assignment and realize that top management believes these tasks are highly visible priorities. With this clear direction, employees understand that they have a common, important objective and that, if their group succeeds, they will be recognized. Interdependence among groups for information and resources to complete their jobs very much affects their interaction.

Values and structures affect the conclusions organizational members make about their relationships with each other. The nature of interpersonal relationships has powerful effects on the coordination of resources needed for organizational effectiveness. Relationships promote decision-making, leadership, and every other aspects of organizational work.

Groups and individuals pursue their self-interests by developing and striving to reach their goals. However, the pursuit of self-interests does not preclude the development of effective collaboration and relationships. Goals may be considered cooperatively, competitively, or independently related. In cooperation, people believe their goal achievements are positively correlated; they can reach their goals to the extent that others also reach their goals. In competition, people believe their goal achievements

are negatively correlated; each perceives that the achievement of one pro-
hibits or at least makes it less likely that others will achieve their goals.
With independent goals, achievements are considered unrelated. Whether
departments understand that their own goals are related cooperatively or
competitively critically affects their expectations, interaction, and outcomes. With cooperative goals, people believe that as one moves toward
goal attainment, others move toward reaching their goals.

Values that create organization-wide respect for the employee's contributions can bind organizational members together and that task interdependence drives team coordination as people clearly recognize that
they need each other's ideas, assistance, and other resources to succeed.
Values of the employees, the structures of task interdependence, and team
procedures that induce cooperative goals among the employees promote
productive interaction. Results support that constructive corporate values
can promote more united organizational efforts. Employees have been
found to value the organization's personal interest in them as people. They
then may reciprocate by feeling part of the organization and its relationships. These bindings to the organization and to the other people lead
them to create effective commitment.

Cross-functional team members are assigned in this Japanese company a common task that appears to lead them to believe that their goals
are cooperative in that they can succeed as the others succeed. The common task is a specific way that they recognize that they must work
together for mutual benefit. They also can appreciate that competitive and
independent efforts will make their own success as well as the success of
other departments less likely. This study provides empirical evidence of
the utility of people, respect values, and interdependent structures and
suggests that cooperative goals mediate their effects on interdepartmental
relationships, which are the ultimate aims for corporate governance and
operations management.

Conclusion

Values are the central elements of management. The purpose of corporate governance is to create appropriate values to promote the effectiveness of the organization. The effectiveness does not mean only profit, but also the loyalty of the workers to promote the organization and the loyalty of the customers to support the organization. In this book, we have examined several Japanese business organizations in a number of countries to examine what kind of organizational culture its corporate governance systems have created.

In this book, we have also analyzed a number of Japanese companies in a number of countries. There are similarities in the management cultures of these companies. The emphasis is on the people, both the customers and the workers. According to the corporate philosophy of Japanese companies, customers and the workers are the most important stakeholders of the company. Thus, the corporate effectiveness means satisfaction of both of these stakeholders.

In normal analysis of corporate governance system so far, there are only descriptions after descriptions. However, in this book we have tried to make the analysis quantitative. The method is to quantify the values of the organizational culture effectively and to analyze their differences and similarities. In this way, we hope the analysis is more interesting to characterize the corporate governance systems.

Decision-making process is defined in terms of creation of a friendly culture in the organization where the values of the employees shaped by their societal values and culture can find a proper home. Organizational culture created by the corporate governance system, which is the product of the national culture, and human resources management practices, creates a synergy, which shapes the fortune of the company's performances. Thus, national culture, organizational values (or purposes), organizational cultures, and corporate performances are interrelated and each depends on the others.

Bibliography

Adler, N. (1991). *International Dimensions of Organizational Behavior.* Boston, MA: PWS-Kent Publishing Company.

Adler, N. & Graham, J. (1989). Cross-cultural interaction: The international comparison fallacy? *Journal of International Business*, 20: 515–537.

Ajzen, I. & Fishbein, M. (1973). Attitudinal and normative variables as predictors of specific behaviours. *Journal of Personality and Social Psychology*, 27: 41–57.

Ajzen, I. & Fishbein, M. (1980). *Understanding Attitudes and Predicting Social Behavior.* Englewood Cliffs, NJ: Prentice Hall.

Albert, S. & Whetten, D. A. (1985). Organizational identity. In *Research in Organizational Behavior.* Cummings, L. L. & Staw, B. M. (Eds.). Vol. 7, pp. 263–295. Greenwich, CT: JAI Press.

Allen, R. F. (1985). Four phases for bringing about cultural change. In *Gaining Control of the Corporate Culture.* R. H. Kilmann *et al.* (Eds.). pp. 332–350. San Francisco: Jossey-Bass.

Allen, R. F. & Dyer, F. J. (1980). A tool for tapping the organizational unconscious. *Personnel Journal*, 59: 192–198.

Arnold, D. R. & Capella, L. M. (1985). Corporate culture and the marketing concept: A diagnostic instrument for utilities. *Public Utilities Fortnightly*, 116: 32–38.

Ashforth, B. E. (1985). Climate formation: Issues and extensions. *Academy of Management Review*, 10: 837–847.

Baltes, B. B., Lacost, H., Parker, C. P., Altmann, R., Huff, J. & Young, S. (1999). A multitrait-multimethod examination of hierarchical models of psychological climate. *Poster session presented at the 14th Annual Meeting of the Society for Industrial and Organizational Psychology,* Atlanta, GA.

Barkema, H., Bell, J. & Penning, J. (1996). Foreign entry, cultural barriers, and learning. *Strategic Management Journal,* 17: 151–166.

Barkema, H. G. & Vermeulen, F. (1997). What differences in the cultural backgrounds of partners are detrimental for international joint ventures? *Journal of International Business Studies,* 28(4) (4th Quarter): 845–864.

Bartlett, C. & Ghosal, S. (1989). *Managing Across the Borders: The Transnational Solution.* Boston, MA: Harvard Business School Press.

Bass, B. & Avolio, B. (1990). *Manual for the Multifactor Leadership Questionnaire.* Palo Alto, CA: Consulting Psychologist Press.

Benerji, K. & Sambharya, R. B. (1996). Vertical 'keiretsu' and international market entry: The case of the Japanese automobile ancillary industry. *Journal of International Business Studies,* 27(1) (1st Quarter): 89–112.

Bernstein, W. M. & Burke, W. W. (1989). Modeling organizational meaning systems. In *Research in Organizational Change and Development.* Woodman, R. W. & Pasmore, W. A. (Eds.). Vol. 3, pp. 117–159. Greenwich, CT: JAI Press.

Beyer, J. & Cameron, K. (1997). Organizational culture. In *Enhancing Organizational Performance.* Washington, DC: National Academy Press.

Bhagat, R. S., Kedia, B. L., Clawford, S. E. & Kaplan, M. (1990). Cross-cultural and cross-national research in organizational psychology: Emergent trends and directions for research in the 1990s. In *International Review of Industrial and Organizational Psychology.* Cooper, C. L. & Robertson, I. T. (Eds.). Vol. 5, pp. 59–99. New York: John Wiley & Sons.

Black, S. J. (1992). Socializing American expatriate managers overseas: Tactics, tenure, and role innovation. *Group & Organization Management,* 17(2): 171–192.

Bluedonn, A. C. (2000). Time and organizational culture. In *Handbook of Organizational Culture and Climate.* Ashkanasy, N. M., Wilderom, C. P. & Peterson, M. F. (Eds.). Thousand Oaks, CA: Sage.

Bluedorn, A. C., Kalliath, T. J., Strube, M. J. & Martin, G. D. (1999). Polychronity and the inventory of polychronic values (IPV): The development of an instrument to measure a fundamental dimension of organizational culture. *Journal of Managerial Psychology,* 14: 205–230.

Borg, I. & Lingoes, J. C. (1987). *Multidimensional Similarity Structure Analysis.* New York: Springer-Verlag.

Borkowski, S. (1999). International managerial performance evaluation: A five country comparison. *Journal of International Business Studies,* 30(3) (3rd Quarter): 533–555.

Brannen, M. Y. (1995). Does culture matters? Negotiating a complementary culture to successfully support technological innovation. In *Engineering in Japan: Japanese Technology Management Practices*. Liker, J. K., Ettlie, J. & Campbell, J. (Eds.). Oxford: Oxford University Press.

Brett, J. M., Tinsley, C. H., Janssens, M., Barsness, Z. I. & Lytle, A. L. (1997). New approaches to the study of culture in industrial/organizational psychology. In *New Perspectives on International Industrial/Organizational Psychology*. Earley, P. C. & Erez, M. (Eds.). pp. 75–129. San Francisco: New Lexington, Press.

Brief, A. P. & Motowidlo, S. J. (1986). Prosocial organizational behaviours. *Academy of Management Review*, 11: 710–725.

Brunsson, N. (1982). The irrationality of action and action rationality: Decisions, ideologies and organization actions. *Journal of Management Studies*, 19: 29–44.

Bryk, A. S. & Raudenbush, S. W. (1992). *Hierarchical Linear Models: Applications and Data Analysis Methods*. Newbury Park, CA: Sage.

Bushe, G. R. (1988). Cultural contradictions of statistical process control in American manufacturing organizations. *Journal of Management*, 14: 19–31.

Buono, A. & Bowditch, J. L. (1989). *The Human Side of Mergers and Acquisitions*. San Francisco: Jossey-Bass.

Calori. R. & Sarnin, P. (1991). Corporate culture and economic performance: A French study. *Organization Studies*, 12(1): 49–74.

Cameron, K. (1986). Effectiveness as paradox. *Management Science*, 32: 539–553.

Cameron, K. (1997). Techniques for making organizations effective: Some popular approaches. In *Enhancing Organizational Performance*. Washington, DC: National Academy Press.

Cameron, K. & Ettington, D. R. (1988). The conceptual foundations of organizational culture. *Higher Education: Handbook of Theory and Research*. pp. 356–396. New York: Agathon.

Cameron, K. S. & Quinn, R. E. (1999). *Diagnosing and Changing Organizational Culture: Based on the Competing Values Framework*. New York: Addison-Wesley.

Campbell, J. P., Brownas, E. A., Peterson, N. G. & Dunnette, M. D. (1974). The measurement of organizational effectiveness: A review of relevant research and opinion. Minneapolis: Final Report, Navy Personnel Research and Development Center, Personnel Decisions.

Campbell, D. T. & Fisk, D. W. (1959). Convergent and discriminant validation by the multitrait-multidimensional matrix. *Psychological Bulletin*, 56: 81–105.

Carlyn, M. (1977). An assessment of the Myers-Briggs type indicator. *Journal of Personnel Assessment*, 45: 461–473.

Carroll, D. T. (1983). A disappointing search for excellence. *Harvard Business Review*, 78–88.

Chatterjee, A. D. (1977). Types of synergy and economic value. *Strategic Management Journal*, 7:119–139.

Choi, F. & Czechowich, I. (1982). *Assessing Foreign Subsidiary Performance*. New York: BIC.

Collet, L. & Mora, C. (1996). MOM data analysis. Working Paper, University of Michigan School of Education and Executive Education Center.

Cook, R. A. & Szumal, J. (2000). Using the organizational culture inventory to understand the operating cultures of organizations. In *Handbook of Organizational Culture and Climate*. Ashkanasy, N. M., Wilderom, C. P. & Peterson, M. F. (Eds.). Thousand Oaks, CA: Sage.

Cooke, R. A. (1997). *Organizational Effectiveness Inventory*. Arlington Heights, IL: Human Synergistics/Center for Applied Research.

Cooke, R. A. & Lafferty, J. C. (1983). *Level V: Organizational Culture Inventory (Form I)*. Plymouth, MI: Human Synergistics.

Cooke, R. A. & Lafferty, J. C. (1986). *Organizational Culture Inventory (Form III)*. Plymouth, MI: Human Synergistics.

Cooke, R. A. & Lafferty, J. C. (1987). *Organizational Culture Inventory*. Plymouth, MI: Human Synergistics.

Cooke, R. A. & Lafferty, J. C. (1994). *Organizational Culture Inventory — Ideal*. Plymouth, MI: Human Synergistics.

Cooke, R. A. & Rousseau, D. M. (1988). Behavioral norms and expectations: A quantitative approach to the assessment of organizational culture. *Group & Organization Studies*, 13: 245–273.

Cooke, R. A. & Szumal, J. L. (1993). Measuring normative beliefs and shared behavioural expectations in organizations: The reliability and validity of the organizational culture inventory. *Psychological Reports*, 72: 1299–1330.

Dansereau, F. & Alutto, J. A. (1990). Level-of-analysis issues in climate and culture research. In *Organizational Climate and Culture*. Schneider, B. (Ed.). pp. 193–236. San Francisco: Jossey-Bass.

Day, D. V. & Bedeian, A. G. (1991). Predicting job performance across organizations: The interaction of work orientation and psychological climate. *Journal of Management Studies*, 17(3): 589–600.

Deal, T. E. & Kennedy, A. A. (1982). *Corporate Culture: The Rise and Rituals of Corporate Life*. Reading, MA: Addison-Wesley.

Denison, D. (1984). Bringing corporate culture to the bottom line. *Organizational Dynamics*, 13(2): 59–76.

Denison, Daniel R. & Mishra, A. K. (1995). Toward a theory of organizational culture and effectiveness. *Organizational Science*, 6(2): 204–223.

DeLima, K. J. (1999). Organizational "C4Q" (the culture and climate for total quality): Consequences and antecedents. Unpublished Doctoral Dissertation. Canterbury, New Zealand: Lincoln University.

Dess, G. G., & Davis, P. S. (1984). Porter's (1980) generic strategies as determinants of strategic group membership and organizational performance. *Academy of Management Journal*, 27(3): 467–488.

De Shon, R. P. & Landis, R. S. (1997). The dimensionality of the Hollenbeck, Williams and Klein (1989) measure of goal commitment on complex tasks. *Organizational Behavior and Human Decision Processes*, 70: 105–116.

Dickinson, M., Aditya, R. & Chokar, J. (2000). Definition and interpretation in cross-cultural organizational culture research: Some pointers from GLOBE research program. In *Handbook of Organizational Culture and Climate*. Ashkanasy, N. M., Wilderom, C. P. & Peterson, M. F. (Eds.). Thousand Oaks, CA: Sage.

D'Iribarne, P. (1997). The usefulness of an ethnographic approach to the international comparison of organizations. *International Studies of Management & Organization*, 26(4): 30–47.

England, G. W. & Lee, R. (1974). The relationship between managerial values and managerial success in the United States, Japan, India, and Australia. *Journal of Applied Psychology*, 59: 411–419.

Ernst, R. C. (1985). Corporate cultures and effective planning: An introduction to the organization culture grid. *Personnel Administrator*, 30: 49–60.

Erramilli, M. (1996). Nationality and subsidiary ownership patterns in multinational corporations. *Journal of International Business Studies*, 26: 225–248.

Etzioni, A. (1975). *An Evaluation of Complex Organizations: On Power, Involvement, and Their Correlates (Rev. Ed.)*, New York: Free Press.

Falkus, S. A. (1998). An assessment of a new organizational culture measure. Unpublished Master's Thesis, University of Queensland.

Finkelstein, S. (1992). Power in top management teams: Dimensions, measurement, and validation. *Academy of Management Journal*, 35: 505–538.

Fitzgerald, T. (1988). Can change in organizational culture really be managed? *Organizational Dynamics*, 17: 4–15.

Friedman, J. (1994). *Cultural Identity and Global Process*. London: Sage.

Frost, P. J., Moore, L. F., Louis, M. R., Lundberg, C. C. & Martin, J. (Eds.) (1991). *Reframing Organizational Culture*. Newbury Park, CA: Sage.

Furnham, A. & Gunter, B. (1993). Corporate culture: Definition, diagnosis and change. In *International Review of Industrial and Organizational Psychology*. Cooper, C. L. & Robertson, I. T. (Eds.). Vol. 8, pp. 233–261. New York: John Wiley & Sons.

Gagliardi, P. (1990). *Symbols and Artefacts: Views of the Corporate Landscape*. New York: de Gruyter.

Geertz, C. (1973). *The Interpretation of Cultures*. New York: Basic Books.

Glaser, R. (1983). *The Corporate Culture Survey*. Bryn Mawr, PA: Organizational Design and Development.

Goldstein, H. (1995). *Multilevel Statistical Models*. London: Edward Arnold.

Gordon, G. G. (1985). The relationship of corporate culture to industry sector and corporate performance. In *Gaining Control of the Corporate Culture*. Kilmann, R. *et al*. (Eds.). San Francisco, CA: Jossey-Bass.

Gordon, G. G. & DiTomaso, N. (1992). Predicting corporate performance from organizational culture. *Journal of Management Studies*, 29: 783–798.

Gordon, M. E., Philpot, J. W., Burt, R. E., Thompson, C. A. & Spiller, W. E. (1980). Commitment to union: Development of a measure and examination of its correlates. *Journal of Applied Psychology Monograph*, 65: 479–499.

Graen, G. B., Hui, C., Wakabayashi, M. & Wang, Z.-M. (1997). Cross-cultural research alliances in organizational research: Cross-cultural partnership-making in action. In *New Perspectives on International Industrial/ Organizational Psychology*. Earley, P. C. & Erez, M. (Eds.). pp. 160–190. San Francisco: New Lexington.

Hanges, P. J. & Dickson, M. W. (2004). Scale development and validation. In *Cultural Influences on Leadership and Organizations: A 62 Nation Study*. House, R. J., Hanges, P. J., Javidan, M. & Dorfman, P. (Eds.). Thousand Oaks, CA: Sage.

Hansen, G. & Wernerfellt, B. (1989). Determinants of firm performance: The relative importance of economic and organizational factors. *Strategic Management Journal*, 10(5): 16–24.

Harris, S. G. & Mossholder, K. W. (1996). The affective implications of perceived congruence with culture dimensions during organizational transformation. *Journal of Management*, 22: 527–547.

Harrison, R. (1975). Diagnosing organization ideology. In *The 1975 Annual Handbook for Group Facilitators*. Jones, J. & Pfeiffer, P. (Eds.). pp. 101–107. LaJolla, CA: University Associates.

Harrison, R. (1979). Understanding your organization's character. *Harvard Business Review*, 57(5): 119–128.

Hatch, M. J. (1997). *Organization Theory and Theorizing: Modern, Symbolic-interpretive and Postmodern Perspectives*. Oxford: Oxford University Press.

Hatch, M. J. (1990). The symbolic of office design. In *Symbols and Artifacts*. Gagliardi, P. (Ed.). New York: de Gruyter.

Hellriegel, D. & Slocum, J. W. Jr. (1974). Organizational climate: Measurement, research, and contingencies. *Academy of Management Journal*, 17: 255–280.

Hennart, J.-F. & Larimo, J. (1998). The impact of culture on the strategy of multinational enterprises: Does national origin affect ownership decisions? *Journal of International Business Studies*, 29(3): 515–538.

Hofstede, G. (1980). *Culture's Consequences: International Differences in Work-related Values*. Beverly Hills, CA: Sage.

Hofstede, G. (1980). *Culture's Consequences*. Newbury Park, CA: Sage.

Hofstede, G. (1991). *Cultures and Organizations: Software of Mind*. Cambridge: McGraw-Hill Book Company.

Hofstede, G. (1993). Cultural constraints in management theories. *Academy of Management Executive*, 7(1): 81–94.

Hofstede, G. (1994). Management scientists are human. *Management Science*, 40: 4–14.

Hofstede, G. (1997). Organization culture. In *The IEBM Handbook of Organizational Behavior*. Sorge, A. & Warner, M. (Eds.). pp. 193–210. London: International Thomson Business Press.

Hofstede, G. & Bond, M. H. (1984). Hofstede's culture dimensions: An independent validation using Rokeach's value survey. *Journal of Cross Cultural Psychology*, 15: 417–433.

Hofstede, G. & Bond, M. H. (1988). The Confucius connection: From cultural roots to economic growth. *Organizational Dynamics*, 16: 5–21.

Hofstede, G., Bond, M. H. & Luk, C. (1993). Individual perceptions of organizational cultures: A methodological treatise on levels of analysis. *Organization Studies*, 14: 483–503.

Hofstede, G., Neuijen, B., Ohayv, D. D. & Sanders, G. (1990). Measuring organizational cultures: A qualitative and quantitative study across twenty cases. *Administrative Science Quarterly*, 35: 286–316.

Hofstede, G. & Peterson, M. F. (2000). National values and organizational practices. In *Handbook of Organizational Culture and Climate*.

Ashkanasy, N. M., Wilderom, C. P. & Peterson, M. F. (Eds.). Thousand Oaks, CA: Sage.

Hooijberg, R. & Petrock, F. (1993). On cultural change: Using the competing values framework to help leaders to a transformational strategy. *Human Resource Management*, 32: 29–51.

House, R. J., Hanges, P. J., Ruiz-Quintanilla, S. A., Dorfman, P. W., Javidan, M., Dickson, M. W. & Gupta, V. (1999). Cultural influences on leadership: Project GLOBE. In *Advances in Global Leadership*. Mobley, W., Gessner, J. & Arnold, V. (Eds.). Vol. 1, pp. 171–233. Greenwich, CT: JAI Press.

House, R. J., Wright, N. & Aditya, R. N. (1997). Cross-cultural research on organizational leadership: A critical analysis and a proposed theory. In *New Perspectives on International Industrial/Organizational Psychology*. Earley, P. C. & Erez, M. (Eds.). pp. 533–625. San Francisco: New Lexington.

Hui, C. H. & Triandis, H. C. (1989). Effects on culture and response format on extreme response styles. *Journal of Cross Cultural Psychology*, 20: 296–309.

Human, J. L. & Berthon, P. (1991). Psychological type, job type and job process: the South African anomaly. *International Journal of Management*, 8(1): 534–543.

Hurley, M. E., Scandure, T. A., Schriesheim, C. A., Brannick, M. T., Seers, A., Vandenberg, R. J. & Williams, L. J. (1997). Exploratory and confirmatory factor analysis: Guidelines, issues and alternatives. *Journal of Organizational Behavior*, 18: 667–683.

Jackson, G. (2003). Corporate Governance, Human Resources Management and Firm Performance. DTI Economic Paper, London: HM Printing Service.

Jick, T. D. (1979). Mixing qualitative and quantitative methods: Triangulation in action. *Administrative Science Quarterly*, 24: 602–611.

Johannensson, R. E. (1973). Some problems in the measurement of organizational climate. *Organizational Behavior and Human Performance*, 10: 118–144.

Jordan, A. T. (1994). Organizational culture: The anthropological approach. In *Practicing Anthropology in Corporate America: Consulting on Organizational Culture*. Jordan, A. T. (Ed.). pp. 3–16. Arlington, VA: American Anthropological Association.

Jöreskog, K. G. & Sörbom, D. (1993). *LISREL 8.03*. Chicago, IL: Scientific Software International.

Jung, C. G. (1923). *Psychological Types*. Harcourt, New York: Brace.

Jung, C. G. (1959). The archetypes and the collective unconscious. In *The collected Works of C. G. Jung*. Vol. 9, Pt.1. Princeton, NJ: Princeton University Press.

Kahle, L. R., Homer, P. M., O'Brien, R. M. & Boush, D. M. (1997). Maslow's hierarchy and social adaptation as alternative accounts of value structures. In *Values, Life-styles, and Psychographics*. Kahle, L. R. & Chiagouris, L. (Eds.). pp. 111–137. Mahwah, NJ: Lawrence Erlbaum Associates.

Kanter, R. (1983). *The Change Masters: Innovations for Productivity in the American Corporation*. New York: Simon & Schuster.

Keen, P. G. & Bronsema G. S. (Eds.) (1981). Cognitive style research: A perspective for integration. *First International Information System Proceedings*, Boston, MA.

Kets de Vries, M. & Miller, D. (1986). Personality, culture, and organization. *Academy of Management Review*, 11: 266–279.

Kilmann, R. H. & Saxton, M. J. (1983). *The Kilmann Saxton Culture Gap Survey*. Pittsburg, PA: Organizational Design Consultants.

Kilmann, R. H. *et al*. (Eds.) (1985). *Gaining Control of the Corporate Culture*. San Francisco: Jossey-Bass.

Kirchmeyer, C. & Cohen, A. (1992). Multicultural groups: Their performance and reactions with constructive conflict. *Group & Organization Management*, 17(2): 153–170.

Kleinberg, J. (1994a). Practical implications of organizational culture where Americans and Japanese work together. *National Association for the Practice of Anthropology Bulletin*, 14: 48–65.

Kleinberg, J. (1994b). Working here is like walking blindly into a dense forest. In *Anthropological Perspectives on Organizational Culture*. Hamada, T. & Sibley, W. E. (Eds.). pp. 153–191. New York: University Press of America.

Kleinberg, J. (1998). An ethnographic perspective on cross-cultural negotiations and cultural production. In *Advances in Qualitative Organization Research*. Wagner, J. A. III (Ed.). Vol. 1, pp. 201–249. Greenwich, CT: JAI Press.

Kluckhohn, C. (1942). Myth and rituals: A general theory. *Harvard Theological Review*, 35: 45–79.

Kluckhohn, C. (1951). Value and value orientations in the theory of action. In *Toward a General Theory of Action*. Parsons, T. & Shils, E. (Eds.). Cambridge, MA: Harvard University Press.

Kluckhohn, F. R. & Strodtbeck, F. L. (1961). *Variations in Value Orientations*. Evanston, IL: Row, Peterson.

Kogut, B. & Singh, H. (1988a). Entering the United States by joint venture. In *Cooperative Strategies in International Business*. Farok, C. & Lorange, P. (Eds.). Lexington, MA: Lexington Books.

Kogut, B. & Singh, H. (1988b). The effect of national culture on a choice of entry mode. *Journal of International Business Studies*, 19: 411–432.

Kotter, J. P. & Heskett, J. L. (1992). *Corporate Culture and Performance*. NY: The Free Press.

Kopelman, R. E., Brief, A. P. & Guzzo, R. A. (1990). The role of climate and culture in productivity. In *Organizational Climate and Culture*. Schneider, B. (Ed.). pp. 282–318. San Francisco: Jossey-Bass.

Kraut, A. I. & Saari, L. M. (1999). Organizational surveys: Coming of age for a new era. In *Evolving Practices in Human Resources Management*. Kraut, A. I. & Korman, A. K. (Eds.). pp. 302–327. San Francisco: Jossey-Bass.

Kravetz, D. (1988). *The Human Resources Revolution*. San Francisco, CA: Jossey-Bass.

Kruskal, J. B. & Wish, M. (1978). *Multidimentional Scaling*. Beverly Hills, CA: Sage.

Larsson, R. & Finkelstein, S. (1999). Integrating strategic, organizational, and human resource perspectives on mergers and acquisitions: A case survey of synergy realization. *Organization Science*, 10(1): 1–26.

Laurence, P. & Lorsch, J. (1967). *Organization and Environment: Managing Differentiation and Integration*. Boston, MA: Harvard University, Division of Research.

Laurent, A. (1983). The cultural diversity of Western management conceptions. *International Studies of Management and Organization*, 13(1–2): 75–96.

Lawrence, J. & Yeh, R. (1995). Individualism and Confucian dynamism: A note on Hofstede's cultural root to economic growth. *Journal of International Business Studies*, 26(3) (3rd Quarter): 655–669.

Levitt, T. (1983). The globalization of the markets. *Harvard Business Review*, 61(3): 92–102.

Lewin, K. (1951). *Field Theory in Social Science*. New York: Harper & Row.

Likert, R. (1961). *New Patterns of Management*. New York: McGraw-Hill.

Likert, R. (1967). *The Human Organization*. New York: McGraw-Hill.

Lubatkin, M., Ndiaye, M. & Vengroff, R. (1997). The nature of managerial work in developing countries: A limited test of the universalist hypothesis. *Journal of International Business Studies*, 28(4) (4th Quarter): 711–733.

Mackenzie, K. (1991). *The Organizational Hologram: The Effective Management of Organizational Change*. Norwell, MA: Kluwer Academic Publishers.

Major, D. A. (2000). Effective newcomer socialization into high-performance organizational cultures. In *Handbook of Organizational Culture and Climate*. Ashkanasy, N. M., Wilderom, C. P. & Peterson, M. F. (Eds.). Thousand Oaks, CA: Sage.

Malinowski, B. (1961). *Dynamics of Culture Change*. New Haven, CT: Yale University Press.

Marcoulides, G. A. & Heck, R. H. (1993). Organization culture and performance: Proposing and testing a model. *Organization Science*, 14(2): 209–225.

Margerison, C. (1979). *How to Assess Your Management Style*. New York: McB Human Resources.

Markus, K. A. (2000). Twelve testable assertions about cultural dynamics and the reproduction of organizational culture. In *Handbook of Organizational Culture and Climate*. Ashkanasy, N. M., Wilderom, C. P. & Peterson, M. F. (Eds.). Thousand Oaks, CA: Sage.

Martin, J. (1995). Organizational culture. In *The Blackwell Encyclopedic Dictionary of Organizational Behavior*. Nicholson, N. (Ed.). pp. 376–382. Cambridge, MA: Blackwell.

Maruyama, M. (1961). *Nihon no Shiso (The intellectual tradition in Japan)*. pp. 123–152. Tokyo: Iwanami Shoten.

Mead, M. (1949). *Coming of Age in Samoa*. New York: William Morrow.

Meyer, P. (2017). Sony's Generic Strategy & Intensive Growth Strategies. Business Management, Panmore Institute.

Mitroff, I. I. & Kilmann, R. H. (1978). Stories managers tell: A new tool for organizational problem solving. *Management Review*, 64: 18–28.

Morishima, M. (1981). *Why Japan has 'Succeeded': Western Technology and Japanese Ethos*. Cambridge: Cambridge University Press.

Myers, I. B. & Briggs, K. C. (1962). *The Myers — Briggs Type Indicator*. Princeton, NJ: Educational Testing Service.

Myers, I. B. & Briggs, K. C. (1980). *Gifts Differing*. Palo Alto, CA: Consulting Psychologists Press.

Nadler, D. A. & Tushman, M. L. (1980). A congruence model for organizational assessment. In *Organizational Assessment: Perspective on the Measurement of Organizational Behavior and the Quality of Working Life*. Lawer, E. E., Nadler, D. A. & Cammann, C. (Eds.). New York: John Wiley & Sons.

Neuijen, B. (1992). *Diagnosing Organizational Cultures: Patterns of Continuance and Change*. Groningen, Netherlands: Wolters-Noordhoff.

Nordstrom, K. (1991). *The Internationalization Process of the Firm. Searching for New Patterns and Explanations*. Stockholm: Institute of International Business, Stockholm School of Economics.

Nutt, P. C. (1988). The effects of culture on decision making. *Omega*, 16(6): 553–567.

Ohmae, K. (1985). *Triad Power: The Coming Shape of Global Competition.* New York: The Free Press.

Okuda, H. (1995). Message from the President, Annual Report of Toyota, Toyota Corporation, Toyota City, Japan.

O'Reilly, C. (1989). Corporations, culture and commitment: Motivation and social control in organization. *California Management Review*, 31: 9–25.

O'Reilly, C. A., III, Chatman, J. A. & Caldwell, D. F. (1991). People and organizational culture: A profile comparison approach to assessing person–organization fit. *Academy of Management Journal*, 34: 487–516.

Ouchi, W. (1981). *Theory Z.* Reading, MA: Addison-Wesley.

Palich, L. E. & Hom, P. W. (1992). The impact of leader power and behavior on leadership perception: A LISREL test of an expanded categorization theory of leadership model. *Group & Organization Management*, 17(3): 279–296.

Pascale, R. T. & Athos, A. G. (1981a). *The Art of Japanese Management.* New York: Simon & Schuster.

Pascale, R. & Athos, A. (1981b). *The Art of Japanese Management.* Harmondsworth: Penguin.

Payne, R. L. (2000). Climate and culture: How close can they get. In *Handbook of Organizational Culture and Climate.* Ashkanasy, N. M., Wilderom, C. P. & Peterson, M. F. (Eds.). Thousand Oaks, CA: Sage.

Peters, T. & Watermann, R. (1982). *In Search of Excellence.* New York: Harper & Row.

Peterson, M., Cameron, K., Spencer, M. & White, T. (1991). *Assessing the Organizational and Administrative Context for Teaching and Learning.* Ann Arbor, MI: NCRIPTAL.

Peterson, R. A. & Jolibert, A. J. P. (1995). A meta-analysis of country-of-origin effects. *Journal of International Business Studies*, 26(4) (4th Quarter): 883–899.

Quinn, R. E. & Cameron, K. (1988). *Paradox and Transformation: Toward a Framework of Change in Organization and Management.* Cambridge, MA: Ballinger.

Quinn, R. E. & Rohrbaugh, J. (1983). A special model of effectiveness criteria: Towards a competing values approach to organizational analysis. *Management Science*, 29: 363–377.

Quinn, R. E. & Spreitzer, G. M. (1991). The psychometrics of the competing values culture instrument and an analysis of the impact of organizational culture on quality of life. In *Research in Organizational Change and Development.* Vol. 5, pp. 115–142. Greenwich, CT: JAI Press.

Ralston, D., Holt, D. H., Terpstra, R. & Kai-Cheng, Y. (1997). The impact of national culture and economic ideology on managerial work values: A study of the United States, Russia, Japan and China. *Journal of International Business Studies,* 1st Quarter: 28(1): 177–207.

Reinolds, P. (1986). Organizational culture as related to industry, position and performance: A preliminary report. *Journal of Management Studies,* 23(3): 333–345.

Rentsch, J. R. (1990). Climate and culture: Interaction and qualitative differences in organizational meanings. *Journal of Applied Psychology,* 75: 668–681.

Rousseau, D. M. (1985). Issues of level in organizational research: Multilevel and cross-level perspectives. In *Research on Organizational Behavior.* Cummings, L. L. & Staw, B. M. (Eds.). Vol. 7, pp. 1–37. Greenwich, CT: JAI Press.

Rousseau, D. M. (1988). The construction of climate in organizational research. In *International Review of Industrial and Organizational Psychology.* Cooper, C. L. & Robertson, I. T. (Eds.). Vol. 3. New York: John Wiley & Sons.

Rousseau, D. M. (1989). Psychological and implied contracts in organizations. *Employee Responsibilities and Rights Journal,* 2: 121–139.

Rousseau, D. M. (1990a). Assessing organizational culture: The case for multiple methods. In *Organizational Climate and Culture.* Schneider, B. (Ed.). pp. 153–192. San Francisco: Jossey-Bass.

Rousseau, D. M. (1990b). New hire perceptions of their own and their employers' obligations: A study of psychological contracts. *Journal of Organizational Behavior,* 11: 389–400.

Rousseau, D. M. (1990c). Normative beliefs in fund-raising organizations: Linking culture to organizational performance and individual responses. *Group & Organization Studies,* 15: 448–460.

Rousseau, D. M. & Cooke, R. A. (1988). Behavioral norms and expectations: A quantitative approach to the assessment of organizational culture. *Group and Organizational Studies,* 13(2): 245–273.

Sashkin, M. & Fulmer, R. (1985). Measuring organizational excellence with a validated questionnaire. Paper Presented at the Annual Meeting of the Academy of Management.

Sathe, V. (1983). Implications of corporate culture: A manager's guide to action. *Organizational Dynamics,* 12: 4–23.

Schein, E. H. (1997). *Organizational Culture and Leadership,* 2nd edn. San Francisco: Jossey-Bass.

Schneider, S. (1985). Strategy formulation: The impact of national culture. *Organizational Studies*, 10: 149–168.

Schneider, B. (1990). *Organizational Climate and Culture*. San Francisco: Jossey-Bass.

Schneider, S. & De Meyer, A. (1991). Interpreting and responding to strategic issues: The impact of national culture. *Strategic Management Journal*, 12: 307–320.

Schweiger, D. M. (1985). Measuring managerial cognitive styles: On the logical validity of the Myers-Briggs type indicator. *Journal of International Business*, 13: 315–328.

Silvester, J., Anderson, N. & Patterson, F. (1999). Organizational culture change: An inter-group attributional analysis. *Journal of Occupational and Organizational Psychology*, 72: 1–23.

Smircich, L. (1983). Concepts of culture and organizational analysis. *Administrative Science Quarterly*, 28: 339–358.

Soutar, G. N., Grainger, R. & Hedges, P. (1999). Australian and Japanese value stereotypes: A two country study. *Journal of International Business Studies*, 30(1) (1st Quarter): 203–216.

Stackman, R. W., Pinder, G. C. & Connor, P. E. (2000). Values lost: Redirecting research on values in the workplace. In *Handbook of Organizational Culture and Climate*. Ashkanasy, N. M., Wilderom, C. P. & Peterson, M. F. (Eds.). Thousand Oaks, CA: Sage.

Thompson, B. & Daniel, L. G. (1996). Factor analytic evidence for the construct validity of scores: A historical overview and some guidelines. *Educational and Psychological Measurement*, 56: 197–208.

Tracey, J. B. & Hinkin, T. R. (1998). Transformational leadership or effective managerial practices? *Group & Organizational Management*, 23(3): 220–236.

Triandis, H. C. (1994). Cross-cultural industrial and organizational psychology. In *Handbook of Industrial and Organizational Psychology*. Triandis, H. C., Dunnette, M. D. & Hough, L. (Eds.). 2nd edn., Vol. 4, pp. 103–172. Palo Alto, CA: Consulting Psychologists Press.

Trice, H. M. & Beyer, J. M. (1985). Using six organizational rites to change culture. In *Gaining Control of the Corporate Culture*. Kilmann, R. H. *et al.* (Eds.). pp. 370–399. San Francisco: Jossey-Bass.

Tzeng, O., Outcalt, D., Boyer, S., Ware, R. & Landes, D. (1984). Item validity of the Myers-Briggs type indicator. *Journal of Personnel Assessment*, 48(3): 255–256.

Van de Ven, A. (1983). Review of in search of excellence. *Administrative Science Quarterly*, 29: 621–644.

Van Maanen, J. (1979). The self, the situation, and the rules of interpersonal relations. In *Essays in Interpersonal Dynamics*. Bennis, W. *et al.* (Eds.). Belmont, CA: Dorsey Press.

Weber, M. (1930). *The Protestant Ethic and the Spirit of Capitalism* (Translated by Parsons, T.). New York: Scribner.

Weber, Y. (1996). Corporate culture fit and performance in mergers and acquisitions. *Human Relations*, 49: 1181–1202.

Weber, Y. (2000). Measuring cultural fit in mergers and acquisitions. In *Handbook of Organizational Culture and Climate*. Ashkanasy, N. M., Wilderom, C. P. & Peterson, M. F. (Eds.). Thousand Oaks, CA: Sage.

Wilderom, C. P., Glunk, U. & Maslowski, R. (2000). Organizational culture as a predictor of organizational performance. In *Handbook of Organizational Culture and Climate*. Ashkanasy, N. M., Wilderom, C. P. & Peterson, M. F. (Eds.). Thousand Oaks, CA: Sage.

Windsor, C. & Ashkanasy, N. M. (1996). Auditor independence decision-making: the role of organizational culture perceptions. *Behavioral Research in Accounting*, 8: 80–97.

Woodcock, M. (1989). *Clarifying Organizational Values*. Brookfield, VT: Gower.

Xenikou, A. & Furnham, A. (1996). A correlational and factor analytic study of four questionnaire measures of organizational culture, *Human Relations*, 49: 349–371.

Yasui, T. (1999). *Corporate Governance in Japan and Its Relevance to the Baltic Region*. Paris: DAF/OECD.

Yeung, A. K., Brockbank, J. Wayne & Ulrich, D. O. (1991). Organizational culture and human resources practices: An empirical assessment. *Research in Organizational Change and Development*. Vol. 5, pp. 59–81. Greenwich, CT: JAI Press.

Zammuto, R. F., Gifford, B. & Goodman, E. A. (2000). Managerial ideologies, organizational culture, and outcomes of innovation: A competing values perspective, In *Handbook of Organizational Culture and Climate*. Ashkanasy, N. M., Wilderom, C. P. & Peterson, M. F. (Eds.). Thousand Oaks, CA: Sage.

Zammuto, R. F. & Krakower, J. Y. (1991). Quantitative and qualitative studies of organizational culture. *Research in Organizational Change and Development*, 5: 84–114.

Zammuto, R. F. & O'Connor, E. J. (1992). Gaining advances manufacturing technology's benefits: The roles of organization design and culture. *Academy of Management Review*, 17: 701–728.

Zikmund, W. G. (1997). *Business Research Methods*, 5th edn. New York, NY: The Dryden Press.

Index